SHAKESPEARE

KING LEAR

NOTES

COLES EDITORIAL BOARD

Publisher's Note

Otabind (Ota-bind). This book has been bound using the patented Otabind process. You can open this book at any page, gently run your finger down the spine, and the pages will lie flat.

Bound to stay open

ABOUT COLES NOTES

COLES NOTES have been an indispensible aid to students on five continents since 1948.

COLES NOTES are available for a wide range of individual literary works. Clear, concise explanations and insights are provided along with interesting interpretations and evaluations.

Proper use of COLES NOTES will allow the student to pay greater attention to lectures and spend less time taking notes. This will result in a broader understanding of the work being studied and will free the student for increased participation in discussions.

COLES NOTES are an invaluable aid for review and exam preparation as well as an invitation to explore different interpretive paths.

COLES NOTES are written by experts in their fields. It should be noted that any literary judgement expressed herein is just that – the judgement of one school of thought. Interpretations that diverge from, or totally disagree with any criticism may be equally valid.

COLES NOTES are designed to supplement the text and are not intended as a substitute for reading the text itself. Use of the NOTES will serve not only to clarify the work being studied, but should enhance the readers enjoyment of the topic.

ISBN 0-7740-3207-3

© COPYRIGHT 2002 AND PUBLISHED BY
COLES PUBLISHING COMPANY
TORONTO - CANADA
PRINTED IN CANADA

Manufactured by Webcom Limited
Cover finish: Webcom's Exclusive **DURACOAT**

CONTENTS

Character Sketches

WILLIAM SHAKESPEARE: LIFE AND WORKS
Biographical Sketch

The Early Years

Despite the scholarship it has generated, our knowledge of Shakespeare's life is sketchy, filled with more questions than answers, even after we discard the misinformation accumulated over the years. He was baptized on April 26, 1564, in Holy Trinity Church, Stratford-on-Avon. As it was customary to baptize children a few days after birth, he was probably born on April 23. The monument erected in Stratford states that he died on April 23, 1616, in his fifty-third year.

William was the third child of John Shakespeare, who came to Stratford from Snitterfield before 1532 as a "whyttawer" (tanner) and glover, and Mary Arden, daughter of a wealthy "gentleman of worship" from Wilmecote. They married around 1557. Since John Shakespeare owned one house on Greenhill Street and two on Henley Street, we cannot be certain where William was born, though the Henley Street shrine draws many tourists each year. William's two older sisters died in infancy, but three brothers and two other sisters survived at least into childhood.

Shakespeare's father was well-to-do, dealing in farm products and wool, and owning considerable property in Stratford. After holding a series of minor municipal offices he was elected alderman in 1565, high bailiff (roughly similar to the mayor of today) in 1568, and chief alderman in 1571. There are no records of young Will Shakespeare's education (though there are many unfounded legends), but he probably attended the town school maintained by the burgesses, which prepared its students for the universities. Ben Jonson's line about Shakespeare's having "small *Latine*, and lesse *Greeke*" refers not to his education but to his lack of indebtedness to the classical writers and dramatists.

On November 27, 1582, a licence to marry was issued to "Willelmum Shaxpere *et* Annam Whateley *de* Temple Grafton." On the next day a marriage bond for "Willm Shagspere" and "Anne Hathwey of Stratford" was signed by Fulk Sandells and John Richardson, farmers of Stratford. This bond stated that there was no "lawful let or impediment by reason of any precontract, consanguinity, affinity, or by any other lawful means whatsoever"; thus "William and Anne (were) to be married together with once asking of the banns of matrimony." The problem of Anne Whateley has led many researchers to argue all kinds of improbabilities, such as the existence of two different Shakespeares and the forging of documents to conceal Shakespeare's true identity. The actual explanation seems to be simple: the clerk who made the marriage licence entry apparently copied the name "Whateley" from a preceding entry, as a glance at the full sheet suggests. (Incidentally, Nicholas Rowe in his life of Shakespeare, published in 1709, well before the discovery of these marriage records, gave Anne's name as Hathaway.) The problems of marriage with Anne Hathaway — he was eighteen and she was twenty-six — and of the bond have caused similar consternation. Why did these two marry when there was such a discrepancy of age? Why only one saying of the banns (rather than the usual three)? Why the emphasis on a possible legal problem? The answer here is not simple or definite, but the birth of a daughter Susanna, baptized at Holy Trinity on May 26, 1583, seems to explain the odd circumstances. It should be recognized, however, that an engagement to marry was considered legally binding in those days (we still have breach-of-promise suits today) and that premarital relations were not unusual or frowned upon when an engagement had taken place. The circumstances already mentioned, Shakespeare's ensuing activities, and his will bequeathing to Anne "my second best bed with the furniture" have suggested to some that their marriage was not entirely happy. Their other children, the twins Hamnet and Judith, were christened on February 2, 1585.

Theatrical Life

Shakespeare's years before and immediately after the time of his marriage are not charted, but rumor has him as an apprentice to a master butcher or as a country teacher or an actor with some provincial company. He is supposed to have run away from whatever he was doing for livelihood and to have gone to London, where he soon joined a theatrical group. At this time there were only two professional houses established in London, The Theatre (opened in 1576) and The Curtain (opened in 1577). His first connection with the theater was reputedly as holder of horses; that is, one of the stage crew, but a most inferior assignment. Thereafter he became an actor (perhaps at this time he met Ben Johnson), a writer, and a director. Such experience had its mark in the theatricality of his plays. We do know that he was established in London by 1592, when Robert Greene lamented in *A Groatsworth of Wit* (September, 1592) that professional actors had gained priority in the theater over university-trained writers like himself: "There is an upstart Crow, beautified with our feathers, that with his *Tygers hart wrapt in a Players hyde,* supposes he is as well able to bombast out a lanke verse as the best of you: and beeing an absolute *Iohannes fac totum* (Jack-of-all-trades), is in his owne conceit the onely Shake-scene in a countrey." An apology for Greene's ill-humored statement by Henry Chettle, the editor of the pamphlet, appeared around December 1592 in *Kind-Hart's Dream.*

Family Affairs

To return to the known details of his family life, Shakespeare's

2

son Hamnet was buried at Stratford on August 11, 1596; his father was given a coat of arms on October 20, 1596; and Will purchased New Place (a refurbished tourist attraction today) on May 4, 1597. The London playwright obviously had not severed connections with his birthplace, and he was reflecting his new affluence by being known as William Shakespeare of Stratford-upon-Avon, in the County of Warwick, Gentleman. His father was buried in Stratford on September 8, 1601; his mother, on September 9, 1608. His daughter Susanna married Dr. John Hall on June 5, 1607, and they had a child named Elizabeth. His other daughter, Judith, married Thomas Quiney on February 10, 1616, without special licence, during Lent and was thus excommunicated. Shakespeare revised his will on March 25, 1616, and was buried on April 25, 1616 (according to the parish register). A monument by Gerard Janssen was erected in the Holy Trinity chancel in 1623 but many, like Milton several years later, protested:

> What needs my *Shakespeare* for his honour'd Bones,
> The labour of an age in piled Stone, . . .
> Thou in our wonder and astonishment
> Hast built thy self a live-long Monument.

Shakespeare's Writings

Order of Appearance

Dating of Shakespeare's early plays, while based on inconclusive evidence, has tended to hover around the early 1590s. Almost certainly, it is his chronicles of Henry the Sixth that Philip Henslowe, an important theatrical manager of the day, referred to in his diary as being performed during March-May, 1592. An allusion to these plays also occurs in Thomas Nashe's *Piers Penniless His Supplication to the Devil* (August, 1592).

The first published work to come from Shakespeare's hand was *Venus and Adonis* (1593), a long poem, dedicated to Henry Wriothesley, Earl of Southampton. A year later *The Rape of Lucrece* appeared, also dedicated to Southampton. Perhaps poetry was pursued during these years because the London theaters were closed as a result of an outbreak of plague. The *Sonnets*, published in 1609, may owe something to Southampton, who had become Shakespeare's patron. Perhaps some were written as early as the first few years of the 1590's. They were mentioned (along with a number of plays) in 1598 by Francis Meres in his *Palladis Tamia*, and sonnets 138 and 144 were printed without authority by William Jaggard in *The Passionate Pilgrim* (1599).

There is a record of a performance of *A Comedy of Errors* at Gray's Inn (one of the law colleges) on December 28, 1594, and, during early 1595, Shakespeare was paid, along with the famous actors Richard Burbage and William Kempe, for performances before the Queen by the Lord Chamberlain's Men, a theatrical company formed the year before. The company founded the Globe Theatre in 1599 and became the King's Men when James ascended the throne. Records show frequent payments to the company through its general manager John Heminge. From 1595 through 1614 there are numerous references to real estate transactions and other legal matters, to many performances, and to various publications connected with Shakespeare.

Order of Publication

The first plays to be printed were *Titus Andronicus* around February, 1594, and the garbled versions of *Henry VI*, Parts II and III in 1594. Thereafter *Richard III* appeared in 1597 and 1598; *Richard II*, in 1597 and twice in 1958; *Romeo and Juliet*, in 1597 (a pirated edition) and 1599, and many others. Some of the plays appear in individual editions, with or without Shakespeare's name on the title page, but eighteen are known only from their appearance in the first collected volume (the so-called First Folio) of 1623. The editors were Heminge and Henry Condell, another member of Shakespeare's company. *Pericles* was omitted from the First Folio although it had appeared in 1609, 1611, and 1619; it was added to the Third Folio in 1664.

There was reluctance to publish plays at this time for various reasons; many plays were carelessly written for fast production; collaboration was frequent; plays were not really considered *reading* matter; they were sometimes circulated in manuscript; and the theatrical company, not the author, owned the rights. Those plays given individual publication appeared in a quarto, so named from the size of the page. A single sheet of paper was folded twice to make four leaves (thus *quarto*) or eight pages; these four leaves constitute one signature (one section of a bound book). A page measures about 6-3/4 in. × 8-1/2 in. On the other hand, a folio sheet is folded once to make two leaves or four pages; three sheets, or twelve pages, constitute a signature. The page is approximately 8-1/2 in. × 13-3/4 in.

Authorized publication occurred when a company disbanded, when money was needed but rights were to be retained, when a play failed or ran into licensing difficulties (thus, hopefully, the printed work would justify the play against the criticism), or when a play had been pirated. Authorized editions are called good quartos. Piratical publication might occur when the manuscript of a play had circulated privately, when a member of a company desired money for himself, or when a stenographer or memorizer took the play down in the theater (such a version was recognizable by inclusion of stage directions derived from an eyewitness, by garbled sections, etc.). Pirated editions are called bad quartos; there are at least five bad quartos of Shakespeare's plays.

Authenticity of Works

Usually thirty-seven plays are printed in modern collections of Shakespeare's works but some recent scholars have urged the addition of two more: *Edward III* and *Two Noble Kinsmen*. At times, six of the generally-accepted plays have been questioned: *Henry I,* Parts I, II and III, *Timon of Athens, Pericles* and *Henry VIII.* The first four are usually accepted today (one hopes all question concerning *Timon* has finally ended), but if Shakespeare did not write these plays in their entirety, he certainly wrote parts of them. Of course, collaboration in those days was common. Aside from the two long narrative poems already mentioned and the sonnets (Nos. 1-152, but not Nos. 153-154), Shakespeare's poetic output is uncertain. *The Passionate Pilgrim* (1599) contains only five authenticated poems (two sonnets and three verses from *Love's Labour's Lost*); *The Phoenix and the Turtle* (1601) may be his, but the authenticity of *A Lover's Complaint* (appended to the sonnets) is highly questionable.

Who Was Shakespeare?

At this point we might mention a problem that has plagued Shakespeare study for over a century: who was Shakespeare? Those who would like to make the author of the plays someone else — Francis Bacon or the Earl of Oxford or even Christopher Marlowe (dead long before most of the plays were written) — have used the lack of information of Shakespeare's early years and the confusion in the evidence we have been examining to advance their candidate. But the major arguments against Shakespeare show the source of these speculators' disbelief to be in classconscious snobbery and perhaps in a perverse adherence to minority opinion. The most common argument is that no one of Shakespeare's background, lack of education, and lack of aristocratic experience could know all that the author knew. But study will reveal that such information was readily available in various popular sources, that some of it lies in the literary sources used for the play, and that Shakespeare was probably not totally lacking in education or in social decorum. The more significant question of style and tone is not dealt with — nor could it successfully be raised. Bacon, for example, no matter how much we admire his mind and his writings, exhibits a writing style diametrically opposite to Shakespeare's, a style most unpoetic and often flat. The student would be wise not to waste time rehashing these unfounded theories. No such question was raised in the seventeenth or eighteenth centuries, and no serious student of the plays today doubts that Shakespeare *was* Shakespeare.

Shakespeare's Plays

Exact dates for Shakespeare's plays remain a source of debate among scholars. The following serve only as a general frame of reference.

COMEDIES	TRAGEDIES	HISTORIES
1591		Henry VI, Part I
1592 Comedy of Errors		Henry VI, Part II
1592 Two Gentlemen of Verona		Henry VI, Part III
1593 Love's Labour's Lost	Titus Andronicus	Richard III
1594		King John
1595 Midsummer Night's Dream	Romeo and Juliet	Richard II
1596 Merchant of Venice		
1596 Taming of the Shrew		
1597		Henry IV, Part I
1598 Much Ado About Nothing		Henry IV, Part II
1599 As You Like It	Julius Caesar	
1599 Merry Wives of Windsor		Henry V
1601 Twelfth Night	Hamlet	
1602 Troilus and Cressida		
1602 All's Well That Ends Well		
1604 Measure for Measure	Othello	
1605	King Lear	
1606	Macbeth	
1607	Timon of Athens	
1607	Antony and Cleopatra	
1608 Pericles		
1609	Coriolanus	
1610 Cymbeline		
1611 Winter's Tale		
1611 Tempest		
1613		Henry VIII

Shakespeare's England

The world of Elizabethan and Jacobean England was a world of growth and change. The great increase in the middle class, and in the population as a whole, demanded a new economy and means of livelihood, a new instrument of government (one recognizing "rights" and changed class structure), a new social code and a broad base of entertainment. The invention of printing a century before had contributed to that broader base, but it was the theater that supplied the more immediate needs of the greatest numbers. The theater grew and along with it came less-educated, more money-conscious writers, who gave the people what they wanted: entertainment. But Shakespeare, having passed through a brief period of hack writing, proceeded to set down important ideas in memorable language throughout most of his career. His plays, particularly the later ones, have been analyzed by recent critics in terms of literary quality through their metaphor, verse-line, relationships with psychology and myth, and elaborate structure. Yet Shakespeare was a man of the stage, and the plays were written to be performed. Only this will fully account for the humor of a deadly serious play like *Hamlet* or the spectacle of a *Coriolanus*.

Life in London

During Shakespeare's early years there, London was a walled city of about 200,000, with seven gates providing access to the city from the east, north and west. It was geographically small and crisscrossed by narrow little streets and lanes. The various wards each had a parish church that dominated the life of the close-knit community. To the south and outside were slums and the haunts of criminal types, and farther out were the agricultural lands and huge estates. As the population increased and the central area declined, the fashionable people of the city moved toward the west, where the palace of Westminster lay. Houses were generally rented out floor by floor and sometimes room by room. Slums were common within the city, too, though close to pleasant enough streets and squares. "Merrie Olde England" was not really clean, nor were its people, for in those days that were no sewers or drains except the gutter in the middle of the street, into which garbage would be emptied to be floated off by the rain. Plague was particularly ravaging in 1592, 1593-94 (when the theaters were closed to avoid contamination) and 1603. Medical knowledge, of course, was slight; ills were "cured" by amputation, leeching and blood-letting. The city was (and still is) dominated by St. Paul's Cathedral, around which booksellers clustered on Paternoster Row.

Religious Atmosphere

Of great significance for the times was religion. Under Elizabeth, a state church had developed; it was Protestant in nature and was called Anglican (or today, Episcopalian). It had arisen from Henry VIII's break with the Pope and from a compromise with the Roman Catholics who had gained power under Mary Tudor.

The Church of England was headed by the Archbishop of Canterbury, who was to be an increasingly important figure in the early part of the seventeenth century. There were also many schismatic groups, which generally desired further departures from Roman Catholicism. Calvinists were perhaps the most numerous and important of the Protestant groups. The Puritans, who were Calvinist, wanted to "purify" the church of ritual and certain ideas, but during the 1590s they were labeled as extremists in dress and conduct.

Political Milieu

During Shakespeare's lifetime there were two monarchs: Elizabeth, 1558-1603, and James I, 1603-1625. Elizabeth was the daughter of Henry VIII and Anne Boleyn, his second wife, who was executed in 1536. After Henry's death, his son by his third wife, Jane Seymour (who died in 1537), reigned as Edward VI. He was followed by Mary Tudor, daughter of Henry's first wife, Catherine of Aragon. Mary was a Roman Catholic, who tried to put down religious dissension by persecution of both Protestants and Catholics. Nor did her marriage to Philip II of Spain endear her to the people.

Elizabeth's reign was troubled by many offers of marriage, particularly from Spanish and French nobles — all Roman Catholic — and by the people's concern for an heir to the throne. English suitors generally cancelled one another out by intrigue or aggressiveness. One of the most prominent was the Earl of Essex, Robert Devereux, who fell in and out of favor; he apparently attempted to take over the reins of control, only to be captured, imprisoned and executed in February, 1601. One claimant to the throne was Mary of Scotland, a Roman Catholic and widow of Francis II of France. She was the second cousin of Elizabeth, tracing her claim through her grandmother, who was Henry VIII's sister. Finally, settlement came with Elizabeth's acceptance of Mary's son as heir apparent, though Mary was to be captured, tried and executed for treason in 1587. Mary had abdicated the throne of Scotland in 1567 in favor of her son, James VI. His ascent to the throne of England in 1603 as James I joined the two kingdoms for the first time, although Scotland during the seventeenth century often acted independently of England.

Contemporary Events

Political and religious problems were intermingled in the celebrated Gunpowder Plot. Angry over fines that were levied upon those not attending Church of England services — primarily Roman Catholics — and offended by difficulties over papal envoys, a group of Catholics plotted to blow up Parliament, and James with it, at its first session on November 5, 1605. A cache of gunpowder was stored in the cellar, guarded by various conspirators, among them Guy Fawkes. The plot was discovered before it could be carried out and Fawkes, on duty at the time, was arrested. The execution of the plotters and the triumph of the anti-Papists led in succeeding years to celebrations in the streets and the hanging of Fawkes in effigy.

Among the most noteworthy public events during these times were the wars with the Spanish, which included the defeat of the Spanish Armada in 1588, the battle in the Lowlands in 1590-1594, the expedition to Cadiz under Essex in 1596 and the expedition to the Azores (the Islands Expedition), also under Essex, in 1597. With trading companies specially set up for colonization and exploitation, travel excited the imagination of the people: here was a new way of life, here were new customs brought back by the sailors and merchants, here was a new world to explore.

8

In all, the years from around 1590 to 1601 were trying ones for English people, relieved only by the news from abroad, the new affluence and the hope for the future under James. Writers of this period frequently reflect, however, the disillusionment and sadness of those difficult times.

The Elizabethan Theater

Appearance

The Elizabethan playhouse developed from the medieval inn with its rooms grouped around a courtyard into which a stage was built. This pattern was used in The Theatre, built by James Burbage in 1576: a square frame building (later round or octagonal) with a square yard, three tiers of galleries, each jutting out over the one below, and a stage extending into the middle of the yard, where people stood or sat on improvised seats. There was no cover over the yard or stage and lighting was therefore natural. Performances were held in the afternoon.

Other theaters were constructed over the years: The Curtain in 1577, The Rose in 1587 (on Bankside), The Swan in 1595 (also Bankside) and Shakespeare's playhouse, The Globe, in 1599 (not far from The Rose). There is still some question about the exact dimensions of this house, but it seems to have been octagonal, each side measuring about 36 feet, with an over-all diameter of 84 feet. It was about 33 feet to the eaves, and the yard was 56 feet in diameter. Three sides were used for backstage and to serve the needs of the players. The stage jutted out into the audience and there was no curtain. The spectators often became part of the action. Obviously, the actors' asides and soliloquies were effective under these conditions.

There was no real scenery and there were only a few major props. Thus the lines of the play had to reveal locations and movement, changes in time or place, etc. In this way, too, it was easier to establish a nonrealistic setting, for all settings were created in words. On either side of the stage were doors, within the flooring were trapdoors (for entrances of ghosts, etc.), and behind the main stage was the inner stage or recess. Here, indoor scenes (such as a court or a bedchamber) were played, and some props could be used because the inner stage was usually concealed by a curtain when not in use. It might also have served to hide someone behind the ever-present arras (hanging tapestry), like Polonius in *Hamlet*. The "chamber" was on the second level, with windows and a balcony. On the third level was another chamber, primarily for musicians.

Actors

An acting company such as the Lord Chamberlain's Men was a fellowship of ten to fifteen sharers with some ten to twelve extras, three or four boys (often to play women's roles) who might become full sharers, and stagehands. There were rival companies, each with its leading dramatist and leading tragic actor and clown. The Lord Admiral's Men, organized in 1594, boasted Ben Jonson and the tragedian Edward Alleyn. Some of the rivalry of this War of the Theaters is reflected in the speeches of Hamlet, who comments on the ascendancy and unwarranted popularity of the children's companies (like the Children of Blackfriars) in the late 1590s.

The company dramatist, of course, had to think in terms of the members of his company as he wrote his play. He had to make use of the physical features and peculiar talents of the actors, making sure, besides, that there was a role for each member. The fact that women's parts were taken by boys imposed obvious limitations on the range of action. Accordingly, we often find women characters impersonating men. For example, Robert Goffe played Portia in *The Merchant of Venice*, and Portia impersonates a male lawyer in the important trial scene. Goffe also played Juliet, and Anne in *Richard III*, and Oberon in *A Midsummer Night's Dream*. The influence of an actor on the playwright can be seen, on the one hand, by noting the "humor" characters portrayed so competently by Thomas Pope, who was a choleric Mercutio in *Romeo*, a melancholic Jaques in *As You Like It*, and a sanguinary Falstaff in *Henry IV*, Part I; and by comparing, on the other hand, the clown Bottom in *A Midsummer Night's Dream*, played in a frolicsome manner by William Kempe, with the clown Feste in *Twelfth Night*, sung and danced by Robert Armin. Obviously, too, if a certain kind of character was not available within the company, then that kind of character could not be written into the play. The approach was decidedly different from ours today, where the play almost always comes first and the casting of roles second. The plays were performed in a repertory system, with a different play each afternoon. The average life of a play was about ten performances.

History of the Drama

English drama goes back to native forms developed from playlets presented at Church holidays. Mystery plays dealt with biblical stories such as the Nativity or the Passion, and miracle plays usually depicted the lives of saints. The merchant and craft guilds that came to own and produce the cycles of plays were the forerunners of the theatrical companies of Shakespeare's time. The kind of production these cycles received, either as moving pageants in the streets or as staged shows in a churchyard, influenced the late sixteenth-century production of a secular play: there was an intimacy with the audience and there was a great reliance on words rather than setting and props. Similar involvement with the stage action is experienced by audiences of the arena theater of today.

The morality play, the next form to develop, was an allegory of the spiritual conflict between good and evil in the soul of man. The *dramatis personae* were abstract virtues and vices, with at least one man representing Mankind (or Everyman, as the most popular of these plays was titled). Some modern critics see *Othello* as a kind of morality play in which the soul of Othello is vied for by the aggressively evil Iago (as a kind of Satanic figure) and passively good Desdemona (as a personification of Christian faith in all men). The Tudor interlude — a short, witty, visual play — may have influenced the subplot of the Elizabethan play with its low-life and jesting and visual tricks. In mid-sixteenth century appeared the earliest known English comedies, Nicholas Udall's *Ralph Roister Doister* and *Gammer Gurton's Needle* (of uncertain authorship). Both show the influence of the Roman comic playwright Plautus. Shakespeare's *Comedy of Errors*, performed in the 1590's, was an adaptation of Plautus' *Menaechmi*, both plays featuring twins and an involved story of confused identities. The influence of the Roman tragedian Seneca can be traced from Thomas Norton and Thomas Sackville in *Gorboduc* to *Hamlet*. Senecan tragedy is a tragedy of revenge, characterized by many deaths, much blood-letting, ghosts, feigned madness and the motif of a death for a death.

Shakespeare's Artistry

Plots

Generally, a Shakespearean play has two plots: a main plot and a subplot. The subplot reflects the main plot and is often concerned with inferior characters. Two contrasting examples will suffice: Lear and his daughters furnish the characters for the main plot of filial love and ingratitude. Gloucester and his sons enact the same theme in the subplot. Lear and Gloucester both learn that outward signs of love may be false. In *A Midsummer Night's Dream*, the town workmen (Quince, Bottom *et al.*) put on a tragic play in such a hilarious way that it turns the subject of the play — love so strong that the hero will kill himself if his loved one dies first — into farce, but this in the main plot is the "serious" plight of the four mixed-up lovers. In both examples Shakespeare has reinforced his points by subplots dealing with the same subject as the main plot.

Sources

The plots of the Elizabethan plays were usually adapted from other sources. Originality was not the sought quality; a kind of variation on a theme was. It was felt that one could better evaluate the playwright's worth by seeing what he did with a familiar tale. What he stressed, how he stressed it, how he restructured the familiar elements — these were the important matters. Shakespeare closely followed Sir Thomas North's popular translation of Plutarch's *Life of Marcus*

Antonius, for example, in writing *Antony and Cleopatra.* He modified Robert Greene's *Pandosto* and combined it with the Pygmalion myth in *The Winter's Tale,* while drawing the character of Autolycus from certain pamphlets written by Greene. The only plays for which sources have not been clearly determined are *Love's Labour's Lost* (probably based on contemporary events) and *The Tempest* (possibly based on some shipwreck account from travelers to the New World).

Verse and Prose

There is a mixture of verse and prose in the plays, partially because plays fully in verse were out of fashion. Greater variety could thus be achieved and character or atmosphere could be more precisely delineated. Elevated passages, philosophically significant ideas, speeches by men of high rank are in verse, but comic and light parts, speeches including dialect or broken English, and scenes that move more rapidly or simply give mundane information are in prose. The poetry is almost always blank verse (iambic pentameter lines without rhyme). Rhyme is used, however (particularly the couplet), to mark the close of scenes or an important action. Rhyme also serves as a cue for the entrance of another actor or some off-stage business, to point to a change of mood or thought, as a forceful opening after a passage of prose, to convey excitement or passion or sentimentality and to distinguish characters.

Shakespeare's plays may be divided into three general categories, though some plays are not readily classified and further subdivisions may be suggested within a category.

The History Play

The history play, or chronicle, may tend to tragedy, like *Richard II,* or to comedy, like *Henry IV,* Part I. It is a chronicle of some royal personage, often altered for dramatic purposes, even to the point of falsifying the facts. Its popularity may have resulted from the rising of nationalism of the English, nurtured by their successes against the Spanish, their developing trade and colonization, and their rising prestige as a world power. The chronicle was considered a political guide, like the popular *Mirror for Magistrates,* a collection of writings showing what happens when an important leader falls through some error in his ways, his thinking or his personality. Thus the history play counsells the right path by negative, if not positive, means. Accordingly, it is difficult to call *Richard II* a tragedy, since Richard was wrong and his wrongness harmed his people. The political philosophy of Shakespeare's day seemed to favor the view that all usurpation was bad and should be corrected, but not by further usurpation. When that original usurpation had been established, through an heir's ascension to the throne, it was to be accepted. Then any rebellion against the "true" king would be a rebellion against God.

Tragedy

Tragedy, in simple terms, means that the protagonist dies. Certain concepts drawn from Aristotle's *Poetics* require a tragic hero of high standing, who must oppose some conflicting force, either external or internal. The tragic hero should be dominated by a *hamartia* (a so-called tragic flaw, but really an *excess* of some character trait, e.g., pride, or *hubris*), and it is this *hamartia* that leads to his downfall and, because of his status, to the downfall of others. The action presented in the tragedy must be recognizable to the audience as real. Through seeing it enacted, the audience has its passion (emotions) raised, and the conclusion of the action thus brings release from that passion (*catharsis*). A more meaningful way of looking at tragedy in the Elizabethan theater, however, is to see it as that which occurs when essential good (like Hamlet) is wasted (through disaster or death) in the process of driving out evil (such as Claudius represents).

Comedy

Comedy in simple terms means that the play ends happily for the protagonists. Sometimes the comedy depends on exaggerations of man's eccentricities — comedy of humors; sometimes the comedy is romantic and far-fetched. The romantic comedy was usually based on a mix-up in events or confused identity of characters, particularly by disguise. It moves towards tragedy in that an important person might die and the mix-up might never be unraveled; but in the nick of time something happens or someone appears (sometimes illogically or unexpectedly) and saves the day. It reflects the structure of myth by moving from happiness to despair to resurrection. *The Winter's Tale* is a perfect example of this, for the happiness of the first part is banished with Hermione's exile and Perdita's abandonment. Tragedy is near when the lost baby, Perdita, cannot be found and Hermione is presumed dead. But Perdita reappears, as does Hermione, a statue that suddenly comes to life. Lost identities are established and confusions disappear but the mythic-comic nature of the play is seen in the reuniting of the mother, Hermione, a kind of Ceres, with her daughter, Perdita, a kind of Proserpina. Spring returns, summer will bring the harvest, and the winter of the tale is left behind — for a little while.

What is it, then, that makes Shakespeare's art so great? Perhaps we see in it a whole spectrum of humanity, treated impersonally, but with kindness and understanding. We seldom meet in Shakespeare a weeping philosopher: he may criticize, but he criticizes both sides. After he has done so, he gives the impression of saying, Well, that's the way life is; people will always be like that — don't get upset about it. This is probably the key to the Duke's behavior in *Measure for Measure* — a most unbitter comedy despite former labels. Only in *Hamlet* does Shakespeare not seem to fit this statement; it is the one play that Shakespeare, the person, enters.

As we grow older and our range of experience widens, so, too, does Shakespeare's range seem to expand. Perhaps this lies in the ambiguities of his own materials, which allow for numerous individual readings. We meet our own experiences — and they are ours alone, we think — expressed in phrases that we thought our own or our own discovery. What makes Shakespeare's art so great, then, is his ability to say so much to so many people in such memorable language: he is himself "the show and gaze o' the time."

Introduction to *King Lear*

Shakespeare's *King Lear* has excited, outraged and confounded critics for more than three hundred years. It is not surprising that such a broad range of emotional reactions coupled with a considerable span of time has led to a great number of written critical appraisals. It is useful to separate the critics' points of view, which fall into three main areas. Some critics see *King Lear* as being pessimistic about man's condition in the world. Others see it as an expression of Christian precepts about evil and salvation. Still others see in it an expression of optimism, however slight.

The pessimists concentrate their attention on the unending flow of tragedy affecting good and evil alike, the comparisons of man with the worst of beasts from the animal world, the apparent hostility of Nature to man, and the repetition of the events in the main plot in the subplot. Perhaps most unbearable to all readers and particularly those who see no ray of hope in the entire play, is Cordelia's death. Samuel Johnson wrote that he was so affected by Cordelia's death he could not reread the play until called upon to do so by his efforts to edit Shakespeare. He wrote:

> . . . Shakespeare has suffered the virtue of Cordelia to perish in a just cause, contrary to the natural idea of justice, to the hope of the reader, and, what is yet more strange, to the faith of the chronicles. . . . A play in which the wicked prosper, and the virtuous miscarry, may doubtless be good, because it is a just representation of the common events of life; but, since all reasonable beings naturally love justice, I cannot easily be persuaded that the observation of justice makes a play worse; or that, if other excellencies are equal, the audience will not always rise better pleased from the final triumph of persecuted virtue.

The pessimistic critics claim there is no justice, no answering voice to Lear's entreaties, no mercy or pity. Gloucester's remark, "As flies to wanton boys are we to the gods; They kill us for their sport" becomes the pessimists' answer to the question about man's nature and a comment on the system of divine justice.

Those who see something other than pure pessimism in the play see Lear's experiences as a purification and his death as a blessed release. The depth of Lear's suffering leads these critics to focus on the similarities between Lear and Christ. "It is impossible to contemplate the death of Lear without thinking of Calvary," wrote J. Dover Wilson. Still others see similarities between Cordelia and Christ. Shakespeare so altered the original versions of Cordelia's happy reunion with her father, that, they say, it was his intention to highlight the symbolism of her death. One critic is convinced that Shakespeare "was unconsciously inspired by a story taken . . . from Christian mythology, with Cordelia in the part of Christ." By her own death she has redeemed her father from his sins. Whether Lear or Cordelia or perhaps both of them together serve as reminders of the sufferings and teachings of Jesus, is not the entire basis of the Christian interpretation of *King Lear*. Perhaps the essential vision of those who see the play in Christian terms is the "peacefulness" with which Lear dies. Lear, they point out, died certain that Cordelia was alive, and so he dies happy. Irving Ribner has stated:

> King Lear asserts the perfection of God's harmonious order and the inevitable triumph of justice, with the forces of evil preying upon and destroying themselves. In the process they subvert the good, but finally good must be victorious.

Closely allied with those who see the play in purely religious terms, are those critics who see a ray of hope at the end of the play that in some way atones for the tremendous suffering of the central characters. This group include those, like Edward Dowden, who view the play in terms of a lesson in stoicism. Dowden said that the play may be viewed optimistically because it details the essential courage and dignity of man.

> The ethics of the play of *King Lear* are stoical ethics. Shakespeare's fidelity to the fact will allow him to deny no pain or calamity that befalls man. . . . He admits the suffering, the weakness of humanity; but he declares that in the inner law there is a constraining power stronger than a silken thread; in the rapture of love and sacrifice, there is a charm which is neither air nor words, but indeed, potent enough to subdue pain and make calamity acceptable.

This is not to say that it was Shakespeare's intention to teach *the* moral truth. Even critics like Dowden admit that there is no single answer to the problem of the play, only different emphases.

A.C. Bradley is another central figure amongst the optimists. He says that *King Lear*'s central theme is found neither in Gloucester's anguished words nor in Edgar's final "the gods are just." Rather, he states:

> Its final and total result is one in which pity and terror, carried perhaps to the extreme limits of art, are so blended with a sense of law and beauty that we feel at last, not depression

and much less despair, but a consciousness of greatness in pain, and of solemnity in the mystery we cannot fathom.

He calls our attention to the extreme instances of good to be found in King Lear's world, claiming that the many instances of love and selfless devotion are equal in number to the examples of evil. Yet we are not moved to question the existence of good in the same way we worry over the presence of evil. "Yet surely, if we condemn the universe for Cordelia's death," he remarks, "we ought also to remember that it gave her birth." The presence of virtue in the world is as much a mystery as the presence of evil; the source and explanation for both is equally unknowable and can, ultimately, be answered only in each person's own heart.

Date of Composition and Sources

According to the title page of the First Quarto, *King Lear* was presented before the King at Whitehall on St. Stephen's night (December 26) in the Christmas holidays, presumably in the year 1606. That quarto was printed by Nicholas Okes for a bookseller named Nathaniel Butter, to be sold in his shop in Paul's churchyard (the yard of St. Paul's Cathedral in London) at the sign of the Pied Bull. Ever since, the First Quarto has been known as the Pied Bull quarto. The date of composition has been debated, but it must have been written after March 1603, the publication date of one probable source — *A Declaration of Popish Impostures* — and before the date of performance at Whitehall. There have been several attempts to connect *King Lear* with historical events of that era, and more than one writer has claimed that its dark mood reflects the Gunpowder Plot of 1605. All of these proposals seem farfetched. The correct date of composition is probably 1605 or early 1606, which would place *King Lear* between *Othello* (1603-4) and *Macbeth* (1606-7).

Shakespeare based the main plot of *King Lear* on a well-known and ancient tale. In the *Historia Regum Britanniae* (1136) by Geoffrey of Monmouth, the earliest known version of the tale, Lear's sons-in-law try to depose him, but he is eventually restored to the throne with the help of the King of France. Lear reigns again as King of England and enjoys Cordelia's love. Later versions of the Lear tale which Shakespeare would have known, such as John Higgins' *The First Part of the Mirrour for Magistrates* (1574), Holinshed's *Chronicles* (1587), Spenser's *Fairie Queene*, and a play written in 1594, but not published until 1605, called *The True Chronicle History of King Lear*, all keep some form of a happy ending. Only with Shakespeare does the Lear tale end on a tragic note — both Lear and Cordelia die.

Shakespeare's source of the subplot is to be found in Sir Philip Sidney's *Arcadia* (1590), Book II, Chapter 10. The old Prince of

Paphlagonia is victimized by his illegitimate son and blinded. His legitimate son, Leonatus, must lead his poor father. The Prince asks to be taken to a high cliff so he might leap to his death but the son refuses. Eventually the old ruler's forces defeat the illegitimate son, the Prince dies, and Leonatus becomes the ruler.

It is evidence of Shakespeare's artistry that he was able to combine the two stories and make one the reflection of the other, thus adding emphasis to the themes in *King Lear*.

Plot Summary

Lear, the powerful ruler of Britain, has decided to divide his great kingdom into three parts, each to be governed by one of his three daughters. He is old and tired and feels that the heavy burdens of state should be passed onto younger shoulders. His two oldest daughters, Goneril and Regan, are already married, Goneril to the Duke of Albany, and Regan to the Duke of Cornwall. Lear's youngest daughter, and favorite, Cordelia, is being courted by both the Duke of Burgundy and the King of France. Lear plans to keep a train of one hundred loyal followers, to be maintained by his daughters, and to spend his remaining years visiting each of them in turn.

Before he gives away his kingdom, however, Lear asks each of his daughters how much they love him. As Goneril and Regan try to outdo each other in exaggerated claims of love and devotion to their father, Cordelia grows more and more troubled, for she is not by nature given to making speeches about her deepest feelings. When her turn comes to answer, she tells Lear that she loves him as a daughter, but when she marries she will, of course, love her husband too. Her honest, forthright reply angers Lear, and in a blaze of wrath, he disowns her, and decides to split his kingdom into two rather than three parts. The Earl of Kent, who understands Cordelia's deep love for her father, tries to dissuade Lear from his rash action, and only succeeds in prodding Lear into such fury that he himself is banished from Britain on pain of death if he should ever return.

When the Duke of Burgundy hears that Cordelia no longer brings a rich dowry with her, he refuses to marry her. But the King of France, who loves her for herself, takes her with him to be his Queen.

Meanwhile, the Earl of Gloucester, a faithful subject of the old king, is having his own problems. He has two sons, Edgar, his legitimate son and heir, and Edmund, a younger and illegitimate child. Edmund hates his brother and plans to dispose of him and seize the title for himself. To do this, Edmund convinces Gloucester by means of a forged letter that Edgar is plotting to kill him to inherit all. Pretending to be a loyal brother, Edmund persuades Edgar to flee the castle. When Edgar cannot be found, Gloucester declares him a hunted outlaw and arranges for Edmund to inherit his title and lands.

During his first visit at the castle of Goneril and her husband, the Duke of Albany, King Lear finds a cold welcome. Annoyed by her father's followers, Goneril instructs her steward, Oswald, to start trouble with Lear's knights so that she may pick a quarrel with her father. Meanwhile the Earl of Kent, disguised as a servingman, attaches himself to Lear's train, despite his banishment, in the hope of protecting the old king from the consequences of his folly.

Goneril and her father quarrel bitterly over the conduct of his 100 knights, and she deprives him of half of them by refusing to pay for their maintenance. In a fury, Lear curses her and leaves with his remaining men for the castle of Regan and her husband, the Duke of Cornwall. Goneril sends a message to her sister telling her of the quarrel. Regan is no more anxious to receive her father than Goneril was. To avoid his visit, she and her husband hurriedly leave their castle and ride to the castle of the Earl of Gloucester.

Kent, still in disguise, is sent as an advance messenger to Gloucester's castle to prepare the way for Lear's train. Kent encounters Oswald before the castle on an errand for Goneril and the two quarrel, almost coming to blows. Regan and her husband are roused by the racket, and put Kent into the stocks for daring to speak his mind before them and insulting Goneril's servant.

When Lear arrives to find his messenger in the stocks, he refuses to believe Regan could be responsible. An angry argument with her follows, but is interrupted by the arrival of Goneril and her husband. Instead of taking Lear's part, Regan greets her sister warmly. The old king is amazed and shocked to find both sisters against him. Regan sides with Goneril and deprives her father of the remainder of his train. Anguished by his two daughters' ingratitude, Lear repents his treatment of Cordelia. Followed only by his faithful jester and the still disguised Kent, he rushes out into a raging winter storm. Regan has the doors barred against him.

Dazed by the power of the storm and stricken by his daughters' treatment, Lear's mind snaps. Kent and the Fool lead him into a dark, miserable hut nearby for shelter, only to find it already occupied. Edgar, instead of fleeing the country, has disguised himself as a wandering madman, "Poor Tom," to escape the savage hunt for him.

News of Lear's plight reaches Gloucester, who has secretly determined to help him. Gloucester has also learned that Cordelia and her husband, the King of France, have landed at Dover with an army to put Lear back on the throne. Gloucester confides all to Edmund who promptly betrays his father to Cornwall and Regan. Gloucester is cruelly blinded despite the efforts of a faithful servant to save him. Cornwall is mortally wounded in the fight, leaving Regan a widow.

Learning of Cordelia's arrival, Kent leads Lear, still raving mad, to Dover and the camp of his daughter Cordelia. Meanwhile, Edgar finds his blinded father wandering over the desolate countryside, and still pretending to be "Poor Tom," he leads his father to safety.

Goneril, contemptuous of her husband for his pity of old Lear, plots to have him killed during the coming battle and marry Edmund, as soon as they have disposed of the threat posed by the French army headed by Cordelia's husband. In the meantime, under Cordelia's loving care, the old king gradually recovers his senses, but their happiness at having found each other again is short-lived. Pressing matters at home suddenly call Cordelia's husband back and the French army is left leaderless.

Just before the battle, Edgar brings an intercepted letter to the Duke of Albany, warning him of his wife's plot. Albany resolves to punish both Edmund and Goneril after the battle, and makes it clear that he intends to restore Lear to the throne after the foreign army has been driven off British soil. Without its leader, the French army is swiftly defeated and, unluckily, Lear and Cordelia fall into Edmund's hands. He sends them off to prison with a secret order that they are to be murdered in their cells. At this point, the widowed Regan, whose forces Edmund has led during the battle, announces her engagement to him. Edmund, it seems, has pledged his love to both sisters.

Albany appears and accuses Goneril and Edmund of treason. She rushes off in hysteria while Edmund is mortally wounded in trial by combat with an unknown challenger, who turns out to be his own brother, Edgar. With his last breath Edmund sends a messenger to stop the murders of Cordelia and Lear. Shortly afterward, the bodies of Goneril and Regan are brought in. Goneril had poisoned her sister earlier to remove her as a rival for Edmund's love and then stabbed herself in despair at the discovery of her crimes. The tragedy comes to an end as Lear carries in the body of Cordelia. The message had been too late to save her. The old king, again mad and broken by grief and remorse, dies over the body of his beloved youngest daughter. In his madness though, he believes he sees Cordelia breathe and come back to life. Thus, he dies happy.

Summaries and Commentaries By Act and Scene

ACT I • SCENE 1

Summary

The play opens in King Lear's palace with a conversation between the Earl of Kent and the Earl of Gloucester. Their remarks reveal the king's intention to divide his land between his sons-in-law. When Edmund, Gloucester's illegitimate son enters, the conversation is interrupted. Gloucester has two sons, Edmund, the illegitimate son and Edgar, the legitimate one. He tells Kent that both sons are equally dear to him.

King Lear, his family and attendants enter with great pomp and ceremony. Lear explains that he wants to withdraw from the affairs of state and leave the ruling of his kingdom to his daughters and their husbands. He will keep for himself only the name of king. He asks his three daughters to tell him how much they love him in order that he may divide his kingdom according to the strength of their love for him. First Goneril, the eldest, and then Regan describe in glowing terms their love for Lear. He is greatly pleased with the profuseness of their expressions of love. Cordelia, the youngest daughter, privately worries about what she will say and decides to "Love, and be silent." When her turn arrives she tells her father she can say nothing to outdo her sisters. Lear, who loves Cordelia most, begs her to speak out. When she does speak she tells her father that she loves him as much as a daughter ought to love her father, no more and no less. Lear is enraged with Cordelia and refuses to hear the sincerity in her words. Instead, he immediately divides her portion of the land between her two sisters and claims he will provide no dowry for her. Her suitors, the King of France and the Duke of Burgundy, must be informed of this change in Cordelia's fortune and so they are sent for immediately.

Kent, Lear's advisor, tells Lear he is acting hastily and with "hideous rashness." He speaks boldly even in the face of Lear's growing anger, citing his love for Lear as his justification. As a result he is banished. Before he leaves, Kent asks the gods to look after Cordelia. He also expresses his hope that the future actions of Goneril and Regan justify their words of love.

Gloucester enters with the King of France and the Duke of Burgundy who are told of Cordelia's newly impoverished state. The King of France, who knew that Cordelia was Lear's favorite, wonders what her offense was to cause such a change in his opinion of her. Cordelia tells him that her only offense was in not speaking with "glib and oily art." Since Cordelia is now out of favor with Lear and brings no dowry with her, the Duke of Burgundy says he is unable to marry

22

her. The King of France, however, declares that Cordelia now seems richer to him than before because he knows that she is virtuous. He agrees to marry her and take her back to France. Cordelia bids her sisters farewell and expresses the hope that they will love their father in spite of her doubts of them. Once Cordelia has departed and Goneril and Regan are left alone on the stage, they discuss their father's weaknesses. They decide that something must be done about him before he treats them the way he has Kent and Cordelia.

Commentary

In the opening scene the stage is set for the central concerns of the play. We meet all of the central characters in the main plot and all of those in the subplot, with the exception of Edgar, who is mentioned but is not present. We are also introduced to a central idea: how do we measure love? Both Lear and Gloucester are tricked into believing themselves loved by those who speak in a flattering way and both reject the children who really do love them.

It is sometimes argued that Lear is mad before the play even opens because of his outrageous logic in dividing his kingdom. An Elizabethan audience with its centralized government and its complete belief in the laws of nature, would have been particularly disturbed with his actions. If not yet mad, Lear is clearly on that road when he dismisses Cordelia for her failure to pass his test. Goneril and Regan easily speak the words they know Lear wants to hear, even though they feel nothing but contempt for him. We soon see that they also easily perform other acts of immoral behavior.

Cordelia's behavior is sometimes considered as inexplicable as Lear's own. Her critics feel her adherence to truth to be too rigid and even in speaking the truth she does not tell Lear the full measure of her love. There is, as Coleridge stated, "some faulty admixture of pride and sullenness in her 'Nothing.'" Yet in stating that she loves Lear "according to her bond" she is saying that she loves him as much as any child could love a father. This is the love due him and this love she freely gives. When Lear turns his back on Cordelia and on her love, he is destroying the natural family unit. His behavior has disrupted the natural law on both state and personal levels.

It is Kent, Lear's trusted and loyal advisor, who points out Lear's dangerous lack of insight. "See better, Lear," he advises. But it is only much later and after a great deal of suffering that Lear does finally begin to see the truth. On the same theme of personal insight, Regan confirms that Lear "hath ever but slenderly known himself," although his present behavior is caused by "the infirmity of his age."

Though certain critics may find fault with Cordelia's behavior, we know that Shakespeare intended her to represent virtue and a spiritual ideal of pure love. The King of France recognizes that she is "most rich, being poor;/Most choice, forsaken; and most lov'd, despis'd." In losing all that she had, Cordelia inherits a better world. Thus Lear did Cordelia "a blessing against his will." This esentially Christian precept is found throughout the New Testament: "Blessed are the meek, for they shall inherit the earth" from the Sermon on the Mount and "Go and sell that thou hast, and give to the poor, and thou shalt have treasure in heaven," Matthew 19:21. The play is, however, essentially pagan in its outlook, perhaps in compliance with a Parliamentary order at that time banning references to "God" on stage.

ACT I • SCENE 2

Summary

Edmund, Gloucester's bastard son, calls upon nature's laws as his guide instead of the laws of society. With both bitterness and humor, he wonders why he should be deprived of all advantages because his parents were not married and because he is a younger son. He decides to use his father's love for him to deprive his brother, Edgar, of his land. He intends to trick his father by means of a letter which he himself has written.

As Gloucester enters, Edmund quite obviously hides the letter. Gloucester, already upset with the events at court, becomes suspicious about the letter's contents. Just as Edmund intended, Gloucester demands to see it. Edmund shows the letter, apparently written by Edgar and outlining a plan for both sons to kill their father and share his lands between them. Gloucester becomes convinced of Edgar's evil intentions and agrees to a plan to eavesdrop on Edgar. Gloucester leaves to await Edward's call. When Edgar enters, Edmund warns him of their father's anger and wonders what Edgar has done to deserve such wrath. Edgar claims there must be a plot against him and then agrees to Edmund's plan to overhear their father's reasons for turning against him. When once again alone on stage, Edmund gloats over the ease with which he is able to deceive both his father and his brother.

Commentary

In his soliloquy, Edmund invokes a Nature very different from the one Lear, Gloucester and Edgar believe in. Edmund's view of nature may appear more sympathetic to us because of his essentially modern outlook. For him Nature is not responsible for man's good fortune or for his misdeeds; Edmund will not allow an unseen entity to take responsibility for what he knows are his own actions. He reasons that man is primarily responsible to himself and that responsibility means he is permitted to employ whatever cunning he may possess to advance his own good fortune. In his system, as in ours, Nature is deaf to any promises or requests.

While much of what Edmund says fits in with our perceptions of the natural world, and while we would agree that custom or tradition could be grossly unfair in its treatment of younger sons and particularly of bastards, it must also be remembered that in Shakespeare's time, Edmund's was not the accepted view. It is true that Hobbes' pessimistic view of the universe was gaining an audience, yet the portrait of Edmund that Shakespeare has drawn is the projection of the modern man.

Edmund mocks his father's beliefs in the traditional universe where the future is revealed in the "eclipses in the sun and moon" and in so doing flaunts another of the traditional precepts, respect of the elderly. His father, however, is not a simple believer in the powers of astronomy. He does acknowledge that the "wisdom of nature" or the natural sciences find no relationship between the physical occurrences of the natural world and man's actions. Yet, he says, certain dire and treacherous actions cannot be otherwise explained.

Gloucester's tragedy is meant to provide an echo of Lear's own and the parallels begin with the word that sets both tragedies in motion: *nothing*. When questioned by her father, Cordelia replies that she can say "nothing." When Gloucester questions Edmund on the contents of the letter, Edmund also replies "nothing" and so the chain of events is set in motion.

Another key image to the play is repeated here. Sight and seeing clearly are often repeated as both Lear and Gloucester are told, in effect, that they lack personal insight and are blind to the faults and virtues of their children. Both Lear and Gloucester do begin to see more clearly during the course of the play although one is mad and the other is physically blind.

In many ways Edgar is the masculine epitome of virtue as Cordelia is the feminine. He is duped by his brother, Edmund, not because of his stupidity, as Edmund tells us, but because of the nobility of his nature. It is beyond him to suspect his brother of treachery.

ACT I • SCENE 3

Summary
In this short scene Goneril instructs her steward, Oswald, to neglect the orders of Lear and his followers as she is angry with her father for striking Oswald. She tells Oswald that Lear is taking liberties in acting that way since he is no longer master or authority but merely an "Idle old man." If, she continues, he does not approve of her treatment, Lear can go to Regan where he will be treated in the same fashion.

Commentary
The primary purpose of this scene is to show Goneril acting upon her earlier exclamation that she and Regan "must do something, an i'

the heat.'' She is choosing to defy the established natural order where fathers and all other older persons are held in esteem and respect. Goneril likens her father's naiveté in thinking he could still remain master after having disposed of his authority to the thoughts of an infant. Yet for all her villainy, Goneril is to some extent justified in her anger. Oswald is not just a servant but a gentleman, the administrator of the estate and responsible for the other servants' behavior. Thus, Lear's striking him could be construed as an insult to not only Oswald but also to Goneril. Furthermore, Goneril is right in stating that it is unfair of Lear to renounce all the authority and problems of kingship and yet still expect to retain all the pleasures of power. Of course, none of these reasons justifies her abhorrent and unnatural treatment of her father.

ACT I • SCENE 4

Summary

Kent enters and expresses his hope that Lear will not recognize him in his disguise but will allow him to become part of his entourage.

When Lear enters he demands his dinner. Kent approaches and asks to serve Lear. As Lear is questioning him about his allegiance, Oswald enters and Lear turns to him and asks about Goneril's whereabouts. Oswald turns his back and walks out on Lear. When a knight enters and Lear tries to question him about Oswald's behavior, the knight replies that Oswald has been behaving most rudely. When Oswald re-enters and again answers Lear in a rude manner, Kent trips him and Oswald falls. Lear is grateful to Kent and accepts his service.

The Fool enters and begins his bitter, though often comic, series of speeches on Lear's foolish behavior. The Fool is acutely aware of the consequences Lear faces in having given over his kingdom to his elder daughters. As if to emphasize his point, Goneril enters, frowning. When Lear questions her about the reason for her sour expression, the Fool notes that there was a time when Lear did not have to worry about his daughter's displeasure. Goneril complains about the behavior of Lear's followers and in particular, of his ''all-licens'd fool.'' Lear cannot believe how Goneril is speaking to him and asks if she is indeed his daughter. She refuses to be embarrassed by his question and continues her criticism of Lear's followers, ending with a request that Lear limit the number of his entourage to 50. Lear is enraged and curses Goneril. Albany enters and begs Lear to have patience, claiming he knows nothing about Goneril's demands. Nonetheless, Lear and his party depart to take up residence with Regan.

Once Lear has left, Goneril asks Oswald to deliver a letter to Regan informing her of what has happened. She tells Albany not to concern himself with her actions as she has a better grasp of politics than he.

Commentary

In this scene Kent is revealed as a man of loyalty and devotion. He determines to follow Lear even though the Fool points out to him that only a fool would follow a dispossessed ruler. Kent, who earlier had realized the relative virtue of Cordelia and her sisters, is also keenly aware of the Fool's insight. "This is not altogether fool, my lord," he tells Lear.

From the moment the Fool enters we are prepared to admire him. Lear greets him fondly with "How now, my pretty knave! how dost thou?" and immediately the Fool begins one of his comic, but ultimately instructive, dialogues with Lear. In fact, it is the Fool who is most active in instructing Lear to "see" better. Under his guidance, Lear comes to realize his own limitations and errors and to better judge the relative merit of others, particularly Cordelia.

Yet for much of the play's history the role of the Fool was missing. Perhaps early audiences found his role in Lear's enlightenment too painful to accept. It is now generally understood that the Fool is Lear's most loyal subject and, along with Kent and Cordelia, most interested in his welfare.

Lear, in this scene, continues to be a man dominated by his emotions, particularly in the venemous outpouring he unleashes against Goneril. Some feel his behavior at this point is not altogether warranted. Perhaps Goneril is right and his knights have been unruly and undisciplined in keeping with Lear's undisciplined behavior as ruler. Then, Goneril is within her rights to request good behavior from his followers. Even if she exaggerates the nature of her complaint, has she, thus far, deserved her father's curse of sterility? Bradley is one of those critics who feels Lear's anger is out of proportion to the offense. Certainly her cruelty becomes increasingly evident and she does later deserve the label of "marble-hearted fiend" and "detested kite" but at this point what is most obvious is Lear's lack of self-control.

If Goneril has not yet deserved the full weight of Lear's curses, her behavior is certainly not commendable. In particular, her criticism of her father's followers demonstrates a lack of compassion and her later objections to her husband Albany's "milky gentleness" betrays her true sentiments. When we learn of the letter she is sending to her sister, we become fully aware of the calculating nature with which she has planned things.

In this scene, Lear is gaining just the faintest glimmer of the consequences of a disordered universe. Nature has been wronged and Lear, in giving away his crown, has lost his identity. "Who is it that can tell me who I am?" he asks. The Fool answers "Lear's shadow," suggesting that the king no longer exists. Lear replies that this is something he must learn, since "by the marks of sovereignty, knowledge, and reason, I should be persuaded I had daughters." Had he indeed followed his sovereignty, knowledge and reason, he would not have been led to the unnatural acts of displacing the daughter who loved him most with her sisters and giving away his authority. He now finds himself in a world where nothing seems natural. Disorderly and insolent servants and an ungrateful daughter are the new order of the day.

As in previous scenes, the word "nothing" figures strongly here. "Can you make no use of nothing?" the Fool asks Lear. "Why no, boy; nothing can be made out of nothing." Yet we see how much has come out of Lear's earlier nothing. Out of nothing has sprung all the tragedy which follows. Lear must eventually face the crushing truth that his tragedy has arisen from his own reply to Cordelia's "nothing." "Nothing will come of nothing" he told her, yet how wrong he was.

Albany, who is presented only briefly in this scene, tries to disassociate himself from Goneril's actions. He appears to be more humane and gentle than she and thus earns her criticism. He helps to demonstrate Goneril's true nature when he wonders how far her "eyes may pierce," suggesting the ferocity of her gaze.

ACT I • SCENE 5

Summary

Kent is sent ahead to Regan with letters informing her of her father's imminent arrival. After Kent has left, the Fool begins chastising Lear for his foolishness in first having given up his kingdom and then for expecting his daughter Regan to behave any differently than Goneril. "She will taste as like this as a crab does to a crab," he tells Lear. Lear tries to listen to the Fool's words but his despair and heartache continually burst forth. A Gentleman arrives to tell Lear that his horses are ready for the journey to Regan's house.

Commentary

This short, transitional scene demonstrates with beautiful clarity and precision Lear's tormented state of mind. We have evidence of Lear trying to keep his mind on what the Fool says, yet we see his mind wandering time and again to the great wrong he did Cordelia, "I did her wrong —," and to the greater wrong done him by his ungrateful daughter, Goneril. "To take 't again perforce! Monster ingratitude!" is his expression of the wish to undo the gift of his kingdom to his thankless daughter. His torments seem to him so great he fears for his very sanity. He senses that having given away so much he is on the threshold of losing all that remains his — his reason.

In this scene the Fool solidifies his role as instructor and prodding conscience to the beleaguered king. The Fool feels he must force Lear to see clearly what his position is and where he has been blind. The truth may be unutterably painful but it must be faced. The Fool can foresee the treatment that Lear will receive at the hands of Regan and tries to prepare Lear for the bitter event. "Shalt see thy other daughter will use thee kindly" he warns Lear, playing with the interpretation of the word "kindly" to mean "after her kind or nature." Lear, perhaps also suspecting the truth, recalls at this instant the wrong he did Cordelia. Cordelia is absent from the stage for most of the play, yet we are never allowed to forget her existence by Lear's frequent oblique references to her and the wrong he has done her.

ACT II • SCENE 1

Summary

Edmund learns that there has been trouble between the Dukes of Cornwall and Albany and that it is likely war will soon be declared. When his informer, Curan, departs, Edmund expresses his excitement at the news. If he moves quickly, he says, he can make this news work to his advantage. He calls Edgar from his hiding place and advises him to flee as their father knows where he is hiding. Edmund asks his brother if he has spoken out against the Duke of Cornwall, as the Duke is on his way. Then Edmund tells Edgar to draw his sword as he must make a show of trying to stop the escape. Edmund is a cunning actor and goes so far as to cut himself in the arm in order to impress his father with the loyalty with which he fought his brother.

Gloucester arrives in response to Edmund's cries and learns that Edmund has been wounded while trying to stop his villainous brother, Edgar. Gloucester does not question Edmund's story and sends his servants after Edgar. Edmund repeats his earlier tale, describing Edgar's wish that Edmund help murder their father. Gloucester believes Edmund and awards him by calling him his "loyal and natural boy" and promising to give him the inheritance which should have been Edgar's.

When Cornwall and Regan enter, they repeat the rumors they have heard about Edgar's behavior. They readily believe Edmund and join forces with Gloucester in condemning Edgar. Cornwall tells Edmund how much he admires his behavior to his father, commending him for behaving as a child should behave to his father. Cornwall then says that Edmond therefore deserves to be accepted as one of Cornwall's trusted followers. Regan then tells Gloucester that the reason for their sudden visit is that she has had some disturbing letters from her sister and her father and decided that she should not be at home until she has decided what course to follow. She asks Gloucester if he will advise her in this situation.

Commentary

Edmund is so cunning that he makes immediate use of information he receives and is able to turn it to his advantage. His audacity is rewarded in this case with the belief that Gloucester, Cornwall and Regan place in him. As we know, his concept of nature embodies the notion that the strong survive and he is determined to be amongst the survivors. Thus, he adapts Curan's information about impending war to his own purposes.

In addition to being an opportunist, Edmund is also an expert manipulator. He manages, in a few words, to convince his father of his loyalty and of Edgar's treachery. He chooses his words carefully, reporting how he tried to stop Edgar by citing how vengeful the gods become about one who commits parricide (one who kills one's parent). Although he himself does not believe in the reactions the gods take to man's misdemeanors, he knows of Gloucester's beliefs. When he later "quotes" Edgar's "Thou unpossessing bastard" he knows he is putting into Gloucester's mind the idea of disinheriting Edgar and appointing himself the new inheritor.

Gloucester may be an innocent victim of Edmund's masterful treachery but he is not merely a foolish old man. He had been the king's trusted advisor. Yet like the king, he has committed an error of judgment in believing himself unloved by those who love him most and loved by those who only look to their own gain. His fault, like Lear's, is that he lacks personal insight and doesn't trust what he knows about his children.

When Regan and Cornwall enter, we do not yet have an exact estimate of their characters. We suspect that Regan is like her sister but her protestations of horror in hearing about Edgar's supposed plan make us wonder. Yet we soon realize her purpose in visiting Gloucester in the middle of the night and with no forewarning. She has cruelly decided not to be at home when her father arrives with his knights. So while commending Edmund's "loyalty" Cornwall and Regan are behaving in a most unbecoming fashion. Also of interest is the quick turn of Regan's mind when she blames Edgar's abominable behavior on the influence of her father's "riotous knights." Like Edmund, she is trying to manipulate Gloucester's reactions to her advantage. She is purposely setting the stage for her story in order to win Gloucester's approval. She asks if he will advise her how to act in light of the quarrel that Goneril and Lear have had. She, like Edmund, is determined to wring an advantage out of the situation.

ACT II • SCENE 2

Summary

The king's messenger, Kent, and Goneril's steward, Oswald, meet outside Gloucester's castle. Kent begins to chastise and berate Oswald for his insulting behavior toward the king. Oswald, however, does not recognize Kent and cannot fathom the reason for such mistreatment. Kent finally gets out his sword and is prepared to duel, but Oswald refuses. Kent then beats him with his sword and Oswald shouts for help. When Edmund arrives with his sword drawn, Kent is prepared to take him on too. Cornwall, Regan and Gloucester all enter and Cornwall forces Edmund and Kent apart. He closely questions Kent on his purpose in beating Oswald and when Kent answers that he had insulted the king, Cornwall determines Kent to be at fault and orders him to be placed in the stocks until noon. Regan amends the order saying that Kent shall remain in the stocks all day and all night. Gloucester, who tries to make Cornwall and Regan change their minds, is disturbed that the king's messenger should be treated with so little respect, but he is unable to convince the others. Before falling asleep, Kent reads a letter he has received from Cordelia who has learned of his disguise.

Commentary

Since we have already been introduced to the loyalty of Kent and the impudence of Oswald, it is easy to side with Kent in his dispute with Oswald. Kent's insight was first made apparent when he tried to dissuade the king from the course of action which resulted in Cordelia's banishment and her sisters' elevation. Now Kent knows that Oswald is in Goneril's service and brings with him letters she has written speaking out against the king. He accuses Oswald of taking "Vanity the puppet's part against the royalty of her father," a reference to the early morality plays where the sins and virtues of man were personified. Here Kent is saying that Oswald is on Goneril's side and is acting against the king. Oswald is a reprehensible, lying coward as he himself makes clear first in his determination not to fight with Kent and then in his lying to Cornwall, Regan and Gloucester about the outcome of the fight. "This ancient ruffian," he said, "whose life I have spared at suit of his gray beard. . ." is his reference to sparing Kent's life out of deference to his age.

Kent's manner is bold and he speaks bluntly. In his defense, he claims to be too old to learn to soften his speech. Yet he does show his ability to speak in courtly phrases when he replies to Cornwall's criticism with "Sir, in good faith, in sincere verity, Whose influence, like the wreath of radiant fire, On flick'ring Phoebus' front. . . ." However, Kent, like Cordelia, refuses to pander to the vanity of the powerful, preferring to state the truth as simply as possible. He takes no pains to conceal his mistrust and dislike of Regan and her husband, a dislike that springs from his recognition of their true sentiments toward Lear.

Cornwall responds to Kent's antagonism by ordering him placed in the stocks. In doing so, Cornwall is not so much insulting Kent himself as indirectly showing his contempt and disdain for the king. Gloucester points this out when he says "The King must take it ill That he, so slightly valued in his messenger, / Should have him thus restrained." Cornwall, and then Regan too, is rebelling against the notion that Lear is still the king and ruler when he puts Kent into the stocks. Cornwall's and Regan's actions demonstrate that Lear is no longer able to command even their respect. They are obviously aligning themselves with Goneril against Lear and the traditional notions of children's respect for their father.

Kent's receipt of a letter from Cordelia has posed problems for some critics who have noted that not enough time has passed for her to learn of Lear's treatment and then reply to it. This is an instance of the playwright's freedom to manipulate time to suit his own purposes, something that is in evidence in many of Shakespeare's plays.

ACT II • SCENE 3

Summary

In this short scene Edgar explains that he avoided those who were sent to capture him by hiding inside a hollow tree. In order to continue eluding his persecutors, he has decided to disguise himself as one of the "Bedlam beggars." These men, also called "Tom o' Bedlams," were lunatic patients who were turned out of the Bethlehem Hospital in order to beg for their food.

Commentary

Edgar's posing as a "poor naked wretch," foreshadows Lear's later madness and concern for all such characters. In choosing to face the storm in his near nakedness he is again offering a premonition of what is soon to befall Lear and Gloucester.

When Edgar concludes with the words "Edgar I nothing am," he is saying that nothing of his former self remains. In the particular choice of words, however, Shakespeare is also reminding us of all the other instances where "nothing" has come to mean so much.

ACT II • SCENE 4

Summary

Lear, the Fool and a Gentleman arrive at Gloucester's castle, wondering at the reason for Regan's hasty departure from her home. While they are pondering this matter, Kent calls to Lear. Kent, who is still in the stocks, is questioned by Lear as to the reason for his appearing in such a shameful position. When Kent tells Lear that Regan and her husband, Cornwall, have set him in the stocks for taking the king's part against Goneril's messenger, Lear is aghast. He is certain there is some error, that Regan could not be so boldly disobedient.

Kent goes on to explain that when he arrived at Regan's castle he was ordered to await a reply. While he waited, Oswald, Goneril's messenger, arrived and received a warm welcome. When Regan and Cornwall read Goneril's letter, they immediately decided to pack up their train and leave their estate, ordering Kent to follow in order to receive a reply to Lear's letter at their leisure. Again Lear is disbelieving. He goes off in search of his daughter.

While Lear is absent, Kent questions the Fool about the diminishing numbers of Lear's train. The Fool explains that when men sense fortune has turned away from their leader they soon desert.

Lear returns accompanied by Gloucester who explains that Regan and Cornwall refuse to see the king as they are tired by their journey. When Lear insists, Regan and Cornwall finally do appear. Lear appeals to Regan's sympathy describing how unkind her sister has been and overlooking the fact of Kent's humiliating punishment. When Regan refuses to sympathize with Lear, and in fact asks him to return to Goneril and ask her forgiveness, Lear is enraged. As he grows angrier, he asks who set Kent in the stocks. When there is no immediate reply, he repeats the question. Just then Goneril arrives and Lear is shocked to see Regan and Goneril embrace. Together they face Lear and, each backing up the demands of the other, tell him that his entourage must be decreased in ever greater numbers. When Regan asks him why he even needs one servant when hers are able to meet his needs, Lear, in an enraged and nearly maddened state, departs the castle.

A great storm begins when Lear leaves the castle and Gloucester, who had followed the king offstage, returns to describe the king's tormented state and the wretched condition of the weather. Regan tells Gloucester to close and bar the doors so that neither Lear nor his loyal, and perhaps desperate, followers may re-enter. "O, sir, to wilful men, / The injuries that they themselves procure / Must be their schoolmasters," she says, implying that Lear will learn his place if made to suffer a little.

Commentary

In this scene we witness the cumulative effect of Lear's grief and rage. When he arrives at Gloucester's castle he is still innocent enough to be puzzled by Regan's sudden absence from home. In the midst of his bewilderment, however, he comes across Kent in the stocks. He cannot believe that Regan, who was to be his refuge from the cruelty of Goneril, could so flaunt her disrespect of him by placing his messenger in the stocks. As Kent recounts his arrival at Regan's and the subsequent arrival of Goneril's messenger, the reasons for her hasty departure become clear to Lear. Yet he still harbors the hope that there has been a misunderstanding. When Regan finally does appear, Lear chooses to ignore the incident of Kent's position in the stocks, and instead focuses on the love he is certain she will show him.

During the preceding events we see Lear's emotional state move from a precarious calm to enraged royalty. When he orders Regan brought before him he is very much the figure of royal authority. When Gloucester tries to make excuses for Regan and Cornwall's absence, referring to the "fiery quality of the Duke" who is "unremovable and fix'd . . . in his own course," Lear's position is undermined. In fact, Gloucester is ascribing to Cornwall the same qualities which characterized Lear when he was still the powerful ruler.

As Lear begins to state his grievances against Goneril and asks for refuge with Regan, his tone changes from one of command to something that closely resembles pleading. His anger is aroused whenever he recalls his treatment at Goneril's hands and he curses her. Yet he tries to control his anger and wheedle his way into Regan's good graces by referring to her "tender-hefted nature" and her eyes which "do comfort and not burn." If Regan should not be glad to see Lear, he says he would "divorce me from thy mother's tomb, / Sepulchring an adultress." Lear is evoking an image here that is contrary to the laws of nature. Lear, who had before violated nature, is now putting his trust in his daughter's compliance with nature's laws. Expecting Regan to sympathize with his position, Lear is putting his faith in Regan's knowing "The offices of nature, bond of childhood" and the duty she owes him. In using the word "bond" to express Regan's position, Lear is repeating the word used by Cordelia who had said she loved her father according to her bond. Lear is beginning to acknowledge the tremendous implications of the words she spoke.

Through this scene our sympathy for the aging ruler comes more and more to the foreground. When he fights with his own rage, trying to contain his anger, first with regard to Kent's ill-treatment and then with Regan and Cornwall's refusal to appear before him, we see in him the beginnings of self-knowledge and restraint. Yet he is unable to restrain himself from cursing Goneril, the pain and humiliation she has caused is more than he can bear. When she appears before him in person he begins to lose the battle with self-control and fears he will soon be mad. "I prithee, daughter, do not make me mad" he asks Goneril.

Goneril and Regan join forces in trying to control their father and the number of his followers. Lear declares his absolute refusal to accept the conditions for his return to Goneril's castle saying he would rather endure "Necessity's sharp pinch" and "abjure all roofs" rather than return with her. Of course, this is just what he does choose to do. We are again offered a glimpse of what will befall Lear.

Perhaps most painful for Lear is the realization that his evil daughters are indeed his own flesh and blood, or as he says, "rather a disease that's in my flesh." He finds he can no longer curse them. Instead, finding within himself some last store of patience, he tells Goneril that it is up to her to choose to change. Of course he still assumes that he will be welcomed at Regan's with his full train. When he learns that she too is denying him, first her love and then, symbolically, his pride and honor which lie in the possession of an entourage, he is no longer able to contain himself. In a speech which shows Lear aligning himself with the poorest among men, he cries:

> O reason not the need! Our basest beggars
> Are in the poorest things superfluous:
> Allow not nature more than nature needs,
> Man's life is cheap as beast's. . . .

Lear is saying that even the poorest of men have some possession they do not really need. If man is allowed only what he needs for simple survival, his life is no different than that of an animal. Lear departs with the sounds of the storm breaking in the background. The storm signifies Lear's own emotional upheaval and the disruption of the natural course which his daughters' rejection denotes.

This scene also serves to solidify the characters of Kent, the Fool and Lear's two daughters. Kent is still the humane, loyal and outspoken moralist we saw him to be in earlier scenes. The Fool also maintains his role of provacateur, chiding not only Lear but also Kent. Through his prompting, Kent realizes that many of Lear's followers have deserted him in the cause of their own self-interest. And although the Fool refuses to accept his own advice to "Let go thy hold when a great wheel runs down a hill, lest it break thy neck with following," he understands the feebleness of most people. Both the Fool and Kent demonstrate not only their love and sympathy for Lear by choosing to stay but also their moral courage.

Not too much needs to be added to our impression of Goneril and Regan. Their behavior allows us to judge them for ourselves. If we had our doubts about Regan's cruelty, these doubts are dispelled when she tells Gloucester to shut tight the door that neither Lear nor his knights might seek refuge from the storm. Cornwall in seconding Regan's order, makes his own position clear.

ACT III • SCENE 1

Summary

While making his way through the storm, Kent comes upon one of Lear's loyal followers who tells him that Lear is raving at the storm accompanied only by his Fool, who is trying, unsuccessfully, to relieve

Lear's madness by jesting with him. Kent informs the Gentleman of the discord between the Dukes of Albany and Cornwall, a discord which threatens to become war. He also tells him that Cordelia and the King of France have been kept informed of the situation in England and of Lear's ill-treatment. France is preparing to invade England and Kent asks the Gentleman to make his way to Dover and inform Lear's loyal followers of the treatment he has received. He also says that when he meets Cordelia he must identify himself with a ring that Kent gives him and she will tell him the name of his informer — who is, of course, Kent. They set off in search of Lear.

Commentary

The primary purpose of this scene is to convey information about Cordelia's imminent return and to offer the suggestion that Lear will be saved and avenged.

Furthermore, the Gentleman's description of Lear's battle with the elements prepares us for the sight we are about to see. It is clear that Lear is becoming mad. His description serves to ease us into the next scene where a shocking vision of a maddened Lear waging war with the storm is presented.

ACT III • SCENE 2

Summary

In the midst of a stupendous storm, Lear stands ranting at the elements. First he says the elements shall do their worst to him since they, unlike his daughters, owe him nothing. Later he says the elements have joined forces with his daughters to battle against an old man. The Fool remains with Lear and tries to get him indoors, telling him to "ask thy daughters' blessing: here's a night pities neither wise men nor fools." Lear ignores him. Lear tries to remain calm, saying "I will be the pattern of all patience; I will say nothing." Yet when Kent approaches, Lear cannot help bursting into another tirade against the forces which threaten his sanity. Kent is able to persuade Lear to enter a hovel that is nearby. Lear, acknowledging that his "wits begin to turn," and that he is feeling cold, enters. Kent announces his intention to return to Gloucester's castle and try to force Lear's daughters to let him in.

Commentary

The Lear in this scene is not the pathetic old man of the previous one. His warring stance against nature and his unnatural daughters lend him an awesome stature and grandness. It is as though in beginning to lose his wits, he is gaining new strength and insight. For the first time his concern is not for himself alone. He threatens all the poor wretches "That hast within thee undivulged crimes" and concludes by accepting his own guilt in his present situation: "I am a man/More sinn'd against than sinning." Although he does admit that he has sinned, his punishment is much more than his sins have warranted. When Kent leads him to the hovel, Lear's concern for the first time extends to his Fool: "Come on, my boy: how dost, my boy? art cold?"

ACT III • SCENE 3

Summary
In private, Gloucester complains to Edmund about the treatment being inflicted upon Lear. When he tried to help Lear, Gloucester says, he was sternly rebuked and threatened. Then Gloucester confides in Edmund that there is a letter he has hidden away that says that part of an army has already landed in England. When Gloucester leaves, Edmund decides to inform Cornwall of the letter. This, he is certain, will mean that his father will lose his lands and he, Edmund, will inherit them.

Commentary
Kent's information about Cordelia's arrival is verified by Gloucester who seems to have received a letter from her. We also see that Gloucester has incurred the anger and suspicion of the daughters and Cornwall by his endeavors to right the wrong done to Lear. When Gloucester, still blind to Edmund's intentions, divulges the contents of the secret letter, the opportunistic Edmund decides to turn in his father. "The younger rises when the old doth fall" he comments upon his treachery.

ACT III • SCENE 4

Summary
Kent leads Lear to the hovel and gently bids him enter. Lear, however, is again so disturbed he claims to not feel the storm. Although he tries to ignore the treatment his daughters have forced upon him, he is unable to shut out all thoughts of their actions. He tells Kent to go indoors, out of the storm, but says he wishes to remain outside to pray. The Fool does go in and Lear speaks to all the homeless wretches of the world, blaming himself for paying too little attention to their condition when he was in the position to do something about it.

The Fool runs out of the hovel warning Lear not to enter as a spirit lives there. Edgar, disguised as poor Tom, enters and Lear converses with him. He asks whether he too has given everything to his daughters. When Kent tries to tell Lear that Tom has no daughters, Lear claims that Kent is lying as nothing else could have reduced a man to such a spectacle. Asking "Is man no more than this?" Lear begins to tear off his own clothes so that he too may be the essence of man.

Gloucester enters, having chosen to disobey Lear's daughters' orders. He has found a place where Lear may be kept fed and warm. Lear refuses to go anywhere without poor Tom, his "noble philosopher."

Commentary

Lear clearly expresses the nature of the torment he suffers. He likens it to the tempest of the elements, claiming that his personal torment drives out all sensation of the physical storm. In the midst of his disturbed state he tries vainly to recapture his sanity, advising himself to "weep no more" and saying he "will endure." He commands himself to not think any more of what his daughters have done: "O, that way madness lies; let me shun that; / No more of that." In ceasing to think about his own situation he becomes newly aware of the plight of the "Poor naked wretches, wheresoe'er you are." Only through his own suffering does he come to realize the suffering of all humanity. Once he is aware, however, there is no more ignoring the problem. He condemns himself for not having done anything to correct the situation when he had the power to do so. "O, I have ta'en / Too little care of this! Take physic, pomp." Lear now feels himself to have a greater kinship with other wretched beings than with his royal daughters. This explains, in part, his reaction to Edgar in his Tom of Bedlam disguise.

When Lear sees the naked and presumably mad beggar, he assumes that he too has given everything to his daughters. In Edgar, Lear sees a man with nothing left to give, a man reduced to an animal existence such as he had described to his daughters in Act II Scene 4, when he cried "Allow not nature more than nature needs, / Man's life is cheap as beast's." Edgar too is an unfortunate victim of injustice, both in Lear's mad eyes and in the more knowledgeable audience's eyes as well. "Thou art the thing itself: unaccommodated man is no more but such a poor, bare, forked animal as thou art" he tells Edgar. Without the trappings of civilized life, the clothing, the perfumes and the social position, man is nothing more than a naked animal. Lear sees no grandness nor grace in humanity.

Edgar describes himself in the lowest terms imaginable. He describes a lustful, sinful character when he is really a symbol of righteousness and virtue. The irony is that almost everyone else in the play is truly as evil as the portrait he paints of himself. As part of his description he calls himself a "hog in sloth, fox in stealth, wolf in greediness, dog in madness, lion in prey." These are references to the traditional animal forms of the classical Seven Deadly Sins, in which man is defined not by his philosophy but by the nature of his animalistic desires.

In this scene we at last see Gloucester's virtue rise up in defense of Lear. In defiance of Lear's daughters' commands he has come to take the king to a safe and warm place. Although the similarities between the plot and the subplot have been apparent for some time, the emphasis is now on the similarity of Lear's and Gloucester's state of mind. "Thou sayest the king grows mad; I'll tell thee, friend, I am almost mad myself." Of course it is most ironic that he speaks these words to Kent, whose predictions of these events he has just quoted, and in the presence of his son Edgar, whom he has rejected.

Edgar's last lines recalling the ballad "Child Rowland and Burd Ellen," have been the subject of much debate. Robert Browning's poem "Childe Roland to the Dark Tower Came" is derived from these lines. When Browning was asked if the basic meaning of his poem was about the nature of stoical endurance, he answered yes. Certainly Edgar, Gloucester and Lear are all emblems of that theme within this play.

ACT III • SCENE 5

Summary

In a brief scene, Edmund tells Cornwall of his father's betrayal. Cornwall rewards Edmund by giving him all of his father's land and title. Cornwall instructs Edmund to locate his father that he might be arrested. Edmund, in an aside, says he hopes that he may find his father offering comfort to the king and thus increase the suspicions against him.

Commentary

Just as Lear was betrayed by his own flesh and blood, so too is Gloucester betrayed by Edmund. This repetition of events increases the feeling of terror and doom that results from the destruction of traditional values. Although seeming to represent a virtuous morality, by revealing Gloucester's supposed treachery, Edmund and Cornwall are demonstrating the true nature of their evil.

ACT III • SCENE 6

Summary

Gloucester leads Lear and his small party to a room in a farmhouse where they can safely remain. Edgar and the Fool continue their prattling, Edgar talks about demons and fiends and the Fool speaking his wise witticisms. Lear decides justice must be fulfilled and his daughters tried for their sins. He appoints Edgar, the Fool and Kent judges and proceeds to charge a piece of furniture, which he calls

Goneril, with her sins. Edgar, overcome with pity for the king, is unable to proceed with his role. Kent urges Lear to lie down and rest, hoping rest will enable him to recall that patience which he had urged upon himself. Lear finally does rest. He has hardly lain down before Gloucester enters with the details of a plot to kill Lear. He urges Kent to quickly take Lear to Dover where sympathetic friends will greet him. As all exit, Edgar remains behind to offer his comments upon the enormity of the king's suffering in comparison with his own. He determines that he too must leave and offers his hopes that the king will safely escape.

Commentary

Lear, who played the role of chief justice in Act I when he meted out reward and punishment to his daughters, now leaves that role to a madman, a Fool and Kent. In a world turned topsy-turvey they are the likeliest candidates for the role. Lear presents his case to them. His daughter, Goneril, kicked her father out. Even his three little dogs have betrayed him, he says, and bark when they see him. As for Regan, Lear wishes to dissect her to see what hard matter has grown around her heart.

After this scene the Fool no longer appears in the play, nor is any explanation given of his whereabouts. In the last act, Lear does mention his poor fool, but it is understood that this is an endearment and refers not to the Fool, but to Cordelia. The Fool disappears from the play because he is no longer necessary. He has teased, prodded and cajoled Lear into a recognition of his own foolishness and helped him reach the wisdom of seeing truly the nature of the men around him. He has also done his best to help Lear retain his sanity, though to little effect. Lear is beyond the point where the Fool's whimsy distracts him. Just as Lear has gone beyond being saved by the Fool's humor, so too has the audience's emotional pitch gone beyond the ability to laugh at the Fool in the midst of Lear's tragedy.

ACT III • SCENE 7

Summary

Cornwall sends Goneril back to Albany with a letter telling of the landing of the French army. In the same breath he orders the arrest of Gloucester who is to be brought to him immediately. Regan suggests Gloucester be immediately hanged but Goneril says his eyes should be plucked out. Edmund is told to accompany Goneril so as not to witness the punishment of his father. Oswald enters and informs Cornwall that Gloucester has alerted the king's party and they have fled to Dover.

Gloucester is brought before Cornwall and Regan who have him tied to a chair and accuse him of treachery. Regan pulls at his beard and Gloucester protests but then owns up to having warned the king to flee to Dover "Because I would not see thy cruel nails Pluck out his poor old eyes; nor thy fierce sister / In his anointed flesh stick boarish fangs." Cornwall punishes Gloucester by plucking out his eye and grinding it with his boot heel. When one of Cornwall's own servants protests the action, Cornwall draws his sword and a brief scuffle ensues in which Cornwall is wounded. The fight ends when Regan stabs the servant from behind. Gloucester's other eye is put out and he is told that Edmund is the one who informed against him. Gloucester realizes then that Edgar has been wronged.

Gloucester is pushed out the castle gates and told to "smell / His way to Dover." One of the servants, however, decides to secretly reach Tom of Bedlam (Edgar) to lead the old earl.

Commentary

This is surely one of the most horrifying scenes in all literature. Had the audience not been carefully prepared by the increasing fury of wickedness that leads up to this scene, it is possible that we would have felt that this action was too extreme. As it is, it is the absolute epitome of evil and an extreme example of the rejection of traditional concerns of loyalty, respect for elders and family ties.

Until the moment of his physical blindness, Gloucester had been morally blind to the virtue in one son and the evil in the other. It is only when he has been blinded in both eyes that he is informed that Edmund is behind his punishment. It is only then that he realizes Edgar's innocence. Yet Gloucester's blindness is not the just punishment of a man who has misjudged his sons. Just as Lear's punishment is far in excess of the crime he committed, so too is Gloucester's. Gloucester has shown himself to be a loyal and even courageous supporter of Lear and when he learns of his error toward Edgar, he immediately asks the gods to forgive him and bless and prosper his legitimate son. He doesn't seek excuses or explanations, he immediately assumes the burden of guilt and asks for forgiveness. Even in the midst of his punishment, when tied to the chair, he speaks truthfully and forcefully about the wickedness of Lear's two daughters. Even then he expresses his certainty that their wickedness will be stopped by "winged vengeance." Gloucester still puts his faith in a moral universe where evil is punished and virtue rewarded. The fact that Cornwall's own servant speaks against the evil done to Gloucester confirms Gloucester's faith in a moral universe. The servant, however, is slain from behind, demonstrating again the awesome power and treachery of evil. Whether or not Gloucester's faith is to be rewarded is still uncertain.

ACT IV • SCENE 1

Summary

Edgar speaks of his situation and expresses the certainty that since he has now reached his lowest point, any change is bound to be for the better. Just as he finishes speaking he sees his father led by an old man. Gloucester tells the man to leave him alone as he is endangering himself by befriending him. Furthermore, he tells him, he has nowhere to go and therefore does not need to see his way. When he had eyes, he says, he still stumbled, now his only wish is to feel the touch of his son Edgar. Edgar, overhearing this, comments that in this uncertain world, one can never say "I have seen the worst."

The old man and Gloucester approach Edgar. Gloucester asks him to lead him to Dover. He explains that there is a cliff there and he wishes to be led to its edge. Edgar agrees to lead him there.

Commentary

In this scene we see Gloucester driven to the edge of sanity. He acknowledges his own hand in his fate, saying "I stumbled when I saw," and determines suicide is the only choice left him. Just as Lear encountered Edgar as he was going mad, so too does Gloucester. Gloucester remembers having seen the Tom o' Bedlam in the storm and recollects that his nakedness and madness had made him think that man was nothing more than a worm. Now his conclusion is even more embittered: "As flies to wanton boys, are we to th'gods, / They kill us for their sport."

There has been much speculation on whether or not Shakespeare intended this to be the final word on the subject of divine justice in the play. If neither Lear nor Gloucester had gained anything from their wretched experiences, perhaps this would be true. But the final curtain has yet to fall and so these lines must be viewed as Gloucester's exclamation of despair.

Just as Lear's torture led him to a deeper realization of the wretched state of all impoverished creatures, Gloucester's newfound insight enables him to speak against the unfair distribution of wealth. "So distribution should undo excess, / And each man have enough," he is moved to say.

It is interesting to note that Edgar does not tell his father his identity even though he has heard Gloucester utter affectionately "O dear son Edgar, / The food of thy abused father's wrath! / Might I but live to see thee in my touch." Edgar instead keeps his father ignorant of his identity until Act V Scene 3 when he admits his error in not informing his father earlier. The only reasonable explanation for his behavior is that structurally it better suited the dramatist to save Gloucester's redemption for the last act.

ACT IV • SCENE 2

Summary

Goneril and Edmund arrive at the Duke of Albany's castle, but Albany does not appear to greet them. Just as Goneril comments on his absence, Oswald enters. He tells Goneril that her husband is a changed man: all the things which should anger him make him smile, while the things which he should find gratifying make him frown. Goneril tells Edmund that her husband's cowardly nature is making him look forward to the invasion by France rather than preparing to bear arms himself. She sends Edmund back to Cornwall to urge him to quickly arm his men while she will busy herself preparing her forces. Before Edmund departs she kisses him and bestows upon him a small gift, declaring her hope that she may soon be his mistress.

Albany enters and harshly criticizes Goneril and her sister for their inhuman treatment of their father. Even an enraged bear would treat him better than these "Tigers, not daughters" have. As Goneril answers, calling him a "milk-liver'd man" and "a moral fool," he is barely able to keep himself from tearing her from limb to limb.

A messenger enters and informs Albany that Cornwall is dead, the victim of a stabbing during the putting out of Gloucester's eyes. Albany is more distressed to learn that Gloucester has been blinded for having dared to serve the king than he is over Cornwall's death. When he hears of the torture inflicted upon Gloucester by Cornwall he feels the heavens are finally delivering appropriate justice in arranging Cornwall's death. Albany is further shocked to learn that Edmund, Gloucester's own son, was party to his father's punishment.

In learning of Cornwall's death, Goneril's first reaction is that now she and Edmund together can gain control of Regan's portion. She then worries that her sister's widowed state may make her more attractive to Edmund.

Commentary

It is only in this scene that Albany finally emerges as a confident moral figure. Goneril may think he is lacking courage since she sees courage as a forceful, brutal and self-interested quality, but the evidence of his moral courage is clear. He is pleased that the forces of France have landed to avenge Lear's ill-treatment, although now that Cornwall is dead, Albany is the ruler of England and will have to bear arms against the invaders. He recognizes the evil in his wife and calls her a "tiger" and a "devil." He is outraged by Edmund's participation in his father's blinding and speaks of revenging Gloucester's torture. He is forceful and energetic and expounds a view of the universe where the offspring that misuses and mistreats a parent "perforce must wither and come to deadly use." Should the world be as Goneril

43

and Edmund see it, with no divine law and none to protest the outrage upon the natural order, then "It will come, / Humanity must perforce prey on itself, / Like monsters of the deep." Of course the news of Cornwall's death provides Albany with immediate confirmation that there are "justicers" to avenge the crimes committed against the natural order.

Goneril's degeneracy is further compounded by her lustful feelings toward Edmund. In a grotesque contrast to the brutality and pain they have shown to Lear and Gloucester, Goneril and Edmund use the language of courtship with each other. Their false chivalry only makes more unbearable the moments of unleashed violence.

ACT IV • SCENE 3

Summary

Kent meets with the Gentleman who tells him that the King of France has had to return to France to take care of some urgent business. The troops will be led by the King's Marshall. When Kent questions the Gentleman about Cordelia's reaction to the letter he had sent describing her father's treatment, the Gentleman describes Cordelia's emotions as "patience and sorrow." She would not allow her emotions to run wild in the presence of others. Kent exclaims that only the influence the stars have on our lives could explain such differences between her and her sisters. Kent then explains that during lucid moments Lear is aware of his surroundings and understands that Cordelia is near. Yet he refuses to see her because he is so ashamed of having "stripp'd her from his benediction" and having given "her dear rights / To his dog-hearted daughters." Kent learns that Albany and Cornwall's forces are on their way to battle. He tells the Gentleman that he will take him to Lear now but that his own identity must remain hidden for a little longer.

Commentary

In the First Folio (1623) this scene was omitted and it has often been argued that there is no real need for the scene at all. While the King of France must be called away, leaving his army without his leadership and so likely to be defeated, this could have been effected briefly in one of the other scenes. With the King of France away, the battle clearly is Cordelia's avenging of her father, rather than a battle between nations.

While the Gentleman's descriptions of Cordelia reminds us of her patience and virtue and prepares us for the eventual reconciliation with her father, this has already been established and is further demonstrated in the last act.

ACT IV • SCENE 4

Summary

Cordelia, now leader of the French forces, consults with a doctor on the remedies that might be used to help her father. He has been seen wandering the fields dressed in wildflowers. As soldiers are sent to find her father, the doctor replies that he might be helped with rest and repose induced with herbs. Cordelia prays he will be found before his rage burns out his life.

When a messenger enters with the news that Cornwall's and Albany's men are approaching, Cordelia answers that her forces are ready. She makes it clear that they are entering into this war not for the sake of acquiring British territory but for her father's sake.

Commentary

Lear's madness has assumed heroic and dangerous proportions. He has become in his suffering larger than life. Thus, it is easy to understand the critics who view him as a Christ-like figure wearing his crown of weeds and bearing the sins of all mankind. The specific weeds mentioned contribute to that interpretation. Rank fumiter, hardocks, nettles and darnel all have either a bitter taste, a burning property or a rank smell and so are fitting symbols of Lear's tortured state. Of course it can be argued equally persuasively that it is really Cordelia who is the figure of salvation. Those critics who believe in her properties of the Saviour point to the speech she makes at the end of this scene: "O dear father,/It is thy business that I go about." S.L. Bethel compares this to the words of Christ found in Luke 2:49: "Knew ye not that I must goe about my father's business." Whether or not this suggestion was intentional on Shakespeare's part, most will agree that Cordelia is the epitome of patience, compassion and spirituality. Unlike Goneril and Edmund, Cordelia has faith in the benevolent and healing properties of nature if it is allowed to flourish untampered. She does not see her sisters' violent, clawing view of things. Even her invasion of England, which she has undertaken on her father's behalf, she sees in benevolent terms. She has come to heal her father and restore his health, sanity and power.

ACT IV • SCENE 5

Summary

Regan discusses with Oswald the imminent war and learns of Albany's reluctant participation. Of more concern to Regan is the letter that Oswald is carrying from her sister to Edmund. She asks Oswald to let her see the letter, saying she suspects her sister of making amorous overtures to Edmund. She informs Oswald that Edmund has agreed to marry her because she is a widow. She gives Oswald another letter for Edmund, who has gone in search of Gloucester. Edmund intends to kill Gloucester because all who see him pity him and criticize those who tortured him. Regan tells Oswald that should he come across Gloucester he is to kill him at once.

Commentary

In this scene we learn that Albany has decided to bear arms against France but it is not clear whether he seeks to defeat the French army or to protect Lear. His conflict is made explicit by Oswald's reference to Goneril as the better soldier.

What is most important in this scene, however, is the evidence of conflict between Goneril and Regan. Their evil has grown and flourished and now seems about to "prey on itself" as predicted by Albany in Act IV Scene 2. The two sisters have become rivals in their love for Edmund and both seem to want to grab the other's share of the kingdom.

ACT IV • SCENE 6

Summary

Edgar tells Gloucester that he has led him to the very edge of the cliff at Dover when in actuality they are standing upon flat ground. Gloucester thanks his son, whom he still believes to be the Tom o' Bedlam. Yet he mentions how much Edgar's speech has changed, the tone and phrasing are now different. Edgar tells him he is mistaken and Gloucester lets the matter rest. He rewards the beggar who has led him to the edge of the cliff with a purse that contains a precious jewel. He bids the beggar farewell and falls off the cliff. Since he is prepared to die, Gloucester actually does faint in his fall. Edgar, now masquerading as a peasant, revives him. He manages to convince Gloucester that he has fallen from a great height and that it is the will of the gods that enabled him to survive such a fall. Furthermore, he tells Gloucester that the fellow that guided him to the brink of the cliff was not a man but a fiend with "a thousand noses" and bumpy horns. Gloucester now believes his life has been spared by the gods and he resolves to patiently endure his afflictions until the time of his natural death.

Lear enters, dressed in the wild weeds and flowers earlier described by Cordelia. His speech is a strange mixture of sense and nonsense. He begins by defending adultery since his legitimate daughters have treated him so evilly while Gloucester's bastard son treated his father so well. Gloucester recognizes the king's voice and tries to kiss his hand. Lear pulls away saying his hand must be wiped clean as "it smells of mortality." Lear describes to Gloucester his impression of the world's justice. It is a system where "Through tatter'd clothes small vices do appear; / Robes and furr'd gowns hide all." Every man is guilty but the rich manage to cloak their sins and escape justice while the poor bear the brunt of the punishment. He concludes by reminding Gloucester that we all enter the world with tears and tears attend our parting too.

One of Cordelia's gentlemen enters leading a search party for Lear. When they try to lead him back to Cordelia he escapes and leads them on a chase. Edgar detains one of the gentlemen and questions him about the coming battle. He is told that the battle is imminent although the queen, Cordelia, has elected to remain behind the main party so that she might help her father. Gloucester prays that he might soon die a natural death so that he might not again be tempted to commit suicide.

Oswald enters and seeing Gloucester attempts to kill him. Edgar, adopting the accent of a man from southern England, tries to stop him. A duel is fought and Oswald is stabbed. As he lies dying Oswald asks Edgar to deliver the letters in his pocket to "Edmund, Earl of Gloucester." Edgar decides to read the enemies' letters in order to learn their plans. He reads the letter from Goneril which contains details of a plot to murder her husband so that she might then marry Edmund. Edgar decides to inform the Duke of Albany of her plan. A drum is heard in the distance and Edgar leads his father off to a safe place.

Commentary

Edgar leads his father to the edge of an imaginary cliff and describes the sight far below. "I'll look no more," he tells his father, "Lest my brain turn, and the deficient sight / Topple down headlong." Edgar implies that his own imperfect sight could make him fall down. In a sense Gloucester has already plunged into the abyss because of his imperfect vision. He suspected his legitimate son of sins which were really to be found in his illegitimate son. His error led to his downfall and he now is so deeply in despair that he believes all men to be little more than animals. As Gloucester prepares to leap off the cliff he kneels to pray to the "mighty gods" whose will he dares not oppose. In order to stop himself from questioning their will, he says he must commit suicide now before his despair drives him to quarrel with their wishes. When he is saved Gloucester interprets it as a sign that the gods have intervened and spared his life. He resolves to stoically endure all his afflictions.

Just then Lear enters and the key figures from the main plot and the subplot meet. Gloucester, blinded and in tattered clothing and Lear, "fantastically dressed with wild flowers" offer a grotesque reflection of each other. The aged, the mighty, the revered have been brought low. And yet Lear asserts that he is still the king, his natural rights are undeniable and so he imagines himself still carrying out his kingly duties: authorizing the minting of coins, giving the soldiers their press-money and inspecting the troops.

When he hears Gloucester's voice, Lear addresses him "Ha! Goneril, with a white beard!" This sets him off on a tale of his daughters' mistreatment of their father. He remembers that before they had received their portions of his kingdom they had agreed with everything he said. Contrary to and in defiance of all laws and natural order, they turned their backs on him. Their behavior has been so unnatural that Lear is justified in believing it possible for Goneril to have grown a white beard.

Lear's voice is recognized by Gloucester who asks if it is the king who is speaking. "Ay, every inch a king," Lear answers. In an ironic speech he demonstrates his power over life and death by forgiving an adulterer. Lust, in this play, is the ever-present symbol of evil and although Lear is mistaken in presuming Gloucester better treated by his illegitimate son than by his legitimate one, his basic premise is that people are not what they seem. The woman who appears to be so virtuous that she shakes her head at the very mention of pleasure, turns out to be the one who is most riotous and lustful. Her virtue is just a pretense. Man, he says, is like a centaur: seemly and proper above the waist and like an animal below. In this image are found both elements of man's nature: he can strive to be thoughtful and rational or he can easily slip into a state of bestiality.

As Lear expounds upon his view of the world's justice, it becomes apparent that there is a great deal of truth and wisdom in his words. Lear explains that in a world of unequal privilege, true justice cannot be found.

The rich and powerful will always be able to hide their sins behind a cloak of respectability while the poor will always be suspected just by virtue of their poverty. Then Lear, who has been counselling himself to be patient, urges that same virtue upon Gloucester. He reminds Gloucester that we are born into the world with tears and with patience must bear our sorrows. Life, on "this great stage of fools" necessitates suffering and that suffering is unavoidable.

Once Lear has led the attendants off on a merry chase, the one Gentleman remains behind to emphasize Cordelia's role. She "redeems nature from the general curse / Which twain have brought her to." Citing this speech, many critics see Cordelia redeeming Lear from "nature" or "Original Sin" and thus, by her death, enabling him to reach salvation. Others believe this to be merely another example of virtue at a moment when the world is seen to be primarily evil.

Virtue is again victorious at the end of this scene when Edgar kills the despicable Oswald, and when Edgar recognizes the true nature of Albany.

ACT IV • SCENE 7

Summary

Cordelia and Kent meet at last and she gratefully acknowledges his loyalty and goodness. She wonders how she shall ever repay him but he says that to be thanked by her is payment enough. When she tells him to change out of his ragged clothes he answers that he has need of his disguise for a little time longer.

The Doctor tells Cordelia that her father, Lear, has had a long sleep and may now be gently awakened. Music starts to play as Lear is carried in. He has been clothed in fresh garments during his sleep. As Lear sleeps Cordelia bends over him and gently kisses him, hoping that her kiss may in some measure repair the wrongs done by her sisters. She speaks feelingly of the torments that her aged father has been made to suffer, remarking that even her enemy's vicious dog would have had a place by the fire during that terrible storm, yet her father was forced to lie in the straw in a hovel with rogues and swine.

As Lear awakens, Cordelia speaks gently to him. Lear's first words are chastisement for whoever it was that saved him from his grave. He doesn't know where he is and is confused even about his own condition. Thinking Cordelia is an angel and himself in purgatory, he kneels before her. She also kneels and asks for her father's blessing. He begs Cordelia not to mock him as he fears he is not in his "perfect mind." He now recognizes Cordelia, but fears that she cannot love him for what he has done to her. She reassures him that she has "no cause, no cause" to hate him. The Doctor warns her not to stir up too many memories of the past as Lear's mind is still in danger. Cordelia, Lear and the Doctor leave together.

Once Lear has been led away, Kent and the Gentleman confer about the coming confrontation. The Gentleman repeats the rumors he has heard about Kent and Edgar's exile in Germany. Kent replies that it is time to ready themselves for the coming battle. When the Gentleman exits Kent realizes that the outcome of the day's battle will determine whether or not his goals have been reached.

Commentary

Since thunder, curses and slamming doors were the accompaniment to Lear's last confrontation with Goneril and Regan, his reconciliation with Cordelia is conducted with gentle and healing music. The warring elements, the chaotic turn nature had taken, is now being restored with the harmony and order that music represents.

Cordelia's great love for her father is amply demonstrated in this tender reunion scene. She truly does feel that she has no cause for anger against her father. Her virtue and goodness have prevented her from ever thinking of her father in ill terms. She has always accepted him, just as she always knew what her relationship to him was and ought to be.

It is her awareness of the tremendous bond between father and daughter that leads her to ask Lear for his blessing. There is no self-conscious play-acting about the love she feels for him.

49

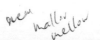

ACT V • SCENE 1

Summary

Edmund and Regan enter with their soldiers. Edmund sends one of the Gentlemen to find out whether Albany's intention to oppose Cordelia's forces still stands. Regan mentions that she is certain Oswald has been killed but Edmund disagrees. Regan's primary concern, however, is not with the battle but with whether or not she has Edmund's love. She questions him closely about his relationship with her sister, Goneril, suspecting they have been intimate. Edmund denies the charge saying he has borne her sister only honorable love. Regan warns him to stay away from Goneril.

Goneril and Albany enter and in a quiet aside, Goneril declares she would rather lose the battle than lose Edmund to Regan. Albany announces his intention to oppose the forces of a foreign invader making it clear, however, that he means no harm to either Lear or Cordelia. Edmund, Goneril and Regan all agree with him. Albany and Edmund agree to meet in a tent to formulate their battle plans. Regan, wanting to keep an eye on her sister, makes Goneril accompany her.

As the group is leaving, Edgar, still in his disguise, quietly approaches Albany and gives him a letter that tells of Goneril's intention to kill Albany. He requests that Albany read the letter before going into battle. Edgar asks that if Albany's forces win and he wishes further evidence of the letter's contents, Albany should let the trumpet sound. Edgar promises to reappear when he hears the trumpet.

Edmund re-enters and tells Albany that Cordelia's army is now very near. He urges him to prepare quickly. When Albany departs, Edmund discusses his relationship with the two sisters. Perhaps he will marry one of them, perhaps neither. In either case Albany will be permitted to help win the battle and then if Goneril wishes to dispose of him, it will be up to her to do so. He also makes it clear that should Lear and Cordelia fall into his hands, he intends to show them no mercy.

Commentary

This scene does little to amplify our knowledge of the characters. Instead, its short, rapid-fire speeches, hurried entrances and exits all prepare us for the final battle and climax. We do learn of Albany's reasons for entering the battle: he is determined to repel the foreign invaders although he means no harm to either Lear or Cordelia.

ACT V • SCENE 2

Summary

In a field between the two camps, a call to battle sounds. Lear,

Cordelia and their forces pass through on their way to engage the enemy. Edgar and Gloucester then enter and Edgar leads his father to a tree for protection during the coming battle. Edgar leaves only to re-enter a moment later with the grim news that Lear and Cordelia have lost the battle and are now prisoners. At this news Gloucester again wishes to lay down and die and Edgar chides him saying it is not for man to determine when he shall leave this earth.

Commentary

The battle is lost and Lear and Cordelia are prisoners. Gloucester again sees the futility in his life and determines to remain where he is, "a man may rot even here," he tells his son. But Edgar will not let Gloucester end his life. He urges a stoic acceptance upon the old man saying "Men must endure/Their going hence, even as their coming hither: / Ripeness is all." Only by living out our allotted years, Edgar says, do we achieve the "ripeness" that makes us ready for the plucking from this world. To take one's own life is to die before the right time. Also suggested by the word "ripeness" is the idea of readiness or preparedness. Only by enduring the whole span of our life do we reach a state of readiness for death. Although Gloucester repeatedly seeks an explanation for his torment, blaming at one time the stars and planets and another time the gods, he learns, as Job did, that there need be no explanation for suffering. The Book of Job, whose echoes are heard throughout this play, is definite about this one point. Job himself rejected the idea that he was being punished for his sins. Instead, comfort must lie in the personal knowledge that we have not done wrong. It was Job who said, "Even though he slay me, yet will I trust him." Now Gloucester too is learning this hard lesson. Although he had earlier referred to the "opposeless wills" of the gods, only now is he really accepting that the gods must determine our "going hence, even as (our) coming hither."

ACT V • SCENE 3

Summary

Edmund enters with Lear and Cordelia as his prisoners. Edmund declares they must be taken away until those in power have determined what is to be done with them. Cordelia is worried over what is now to happen to her father but Lear is content just to be with Cordelia.

As they are taken away, Edmund calls to a Captain and gives him a message with instructions that are to be strictly followed. If the Captain carries out these orders, Edmund assures him he will receive just reward. The Captain agrees and exits.

Albany, Goneril, Regan and their company enter and immediately

Albany demands Edmund deliver Lear and Cordelia into his safe keeping. Edmund replies that he thinks it best if Lear and Cordelia remain in prison until the following day when it will be more fitting to sentence them to their fates. Albany is outraged that Edmund has taken it upon himself to make such decisions and reminds him that he is not a commander but a subject. When Regan speaks up for Edmund saying she wants him to be her husband, Goneril enters into a bitter argument with her sister. Albany then tells Edmund that he and Goneril are under arrest for treason. He bitterly informs Regan that she cannot marry Edmund as he is already contracted to marry his own wife, Goneril.

Albany orders the trumpet sounded to call forward the man who can prove his charges against Edmund. Regan cries out that she is sick. In an aside, Goneril declares that if Regan is not truly sick, she will never again trust poison, thus indicating that she poisoned her sister. Albany states that should no one appear to prove the charges against Edmund he himself will duel with him unto death. A herald approaches to sound the trumpet and Regan, grown increasingly ill, is carried off to Albany's tent.

At the third sound of the trumpet, Edgar appears well disguised in armor, and challenges Edmund. He accuses him of being a "traitor; / False to thy god, thy brother, and thy father; / Conspirant 'gainst this high-illustrious prince. . . ." They fight and Edmund falls wounded.

Once Edmund has been defeated, Goneril claims he has been tricked and did not have to fight an unnamed opponent. When Albany charges her with her part in the treasonous plan, she declares that she makes the laws and therefore there is no man who can charge her with a crime. She exits and Albany sends a soldier after her.

Edgar reveals himself to his brother and Albany. With great feeling Edgar describes his father's suffering. He tells them that he finally revealed his identity to his father because he did not know the outcome of the anticipated duel with Edmund. His father, Gloucester, weakened by his experiences, was unable to endure the joy of finding his son and he died, his heart "'Twixt two extremes of passion, joy and grief, / Burst smilingly." Edgar goes on to describe the arrival of Kent on the scene in his ragged clothes. He says that Kent was so grief-stricken with the suffering Lear was forced to endure that in recounting the tale he fell into a trance of despair. At this point a Gentleman enters with a bloody knife declaring that Goneril has taken her own life and Regan is dead, poisoned by Goneril. Albany orders the bodies be brought forward.

Kent enters and says he wishes to bid farewell to his master, Lear. As Edmund lies dying he determines to try and do some good before his death and informs the others of his plot against Lear and Cordelia. Edgar rushes out to stop the executions, but he is too late.

Lear enters carrying Cordelia in his arms. She is dead and his grief knows no words. Kent reveals himself to Lear but Lear's great grief has again unhinged his mind. He dies thinking he sees Cordelia begin to breathe.

Albany resigns from his office, turning the reins of state over to Kent and Edgar but Kent declares that he too is dying and will not live to rule. Edgar speaks the final lines which emphasize the importance of speaking the truth. He affirms that the young will never "see so much, nor live so long" as their fathers.

The First Quarto has Albany reciting these final lines. Later versions of the play give this speech to Edgar, as he is the young hero, about to assume the reins of office and his role is thus judged more important.

Commentary

In this monumental scene Shakespeare brings together all the elements of plot and subplot. The resolution of the subplot with Gloucester's death prepares us in some way for the multiple tragedies that follow. Yet nothing can adequately prepare us for the pitilessness of the gods who have rewarded both deserving and undeserving with death.

Edgar had earlier described his motives for not revealing his true identity to his father. He wanted to win his father from his despair. Yet it seems likely Gloucester could have better endured his sufferings had he known his son was with him and had freely forgiven him his earlier accusations. And if the old Earl had been converted to Edgar's belief that "Ripeness is all" his belief would again have been sorely tested with Cordelia's untimely and unjust death. No, the only comfort to be found in Gloucester's death seems to lie in ascribing to him the true vision he so sorely lacked when he had use of both his eyes.

Cordelia's first words in this scene — "We are not the first / Who with the best meaning have incurr'd the worst" — bring to mind again the ordeal of Job. She recognizes that reward and punishment do not necessarily follow our actions. Her good intentions have brought her father to prison and herself, although she does not yet know it, to death. She asks Lear if they should see "these daughters and these sisters" who have brought them to this state. She divorces herself as much as possible from her sisters by saying "these" instead of "my sisters." In his reply, Lear also emphasizes the distance between the virtuous and the evil. "No, no, no, no!" he says as though trying to negate the very connection between himself, Cordelia and the evil daughters he has spawned. Lear paints a rosy picture of the life he and Cordelia will live in prison. They will "sing like birds i' th' cage" so great will their happiness be. Having each other and having love will be enough to transform their prison into a haven. Lear also swears not to forget the lessons in humility he has learned. He says they will "take upon 's the mystery of things, / As if we were God's spies." Having each other, he and Cordelia will have all.

In condemning Lear and Cordelia to death, Edmund is acting true to his own self-interested nature. His subsequent behavior, when he tries to revoke the evil he has set into motion, requires explanation.

After Edmund is wounded by Edgar, he wishes to know whether or not his challenger is of noble birth. He has risen so high from such low beginnings, that it is now of utmost importance to him that his slayer be of noble birth. When it is revealed that it is his own brother who has stabbed him, he says that the wheel of fortune has come full circle and he agrees with Edgar's claim that he is now in the "dark and vicious place" here he was conceived. Edmund has readily confessed his treacheries. He has always acted on the principle of self-interest and now that there is nothing to be gained, he holds nothing back. Yet the great turning point where he actually desires to do something good has not yet been reached. Only after Goneril and Regan are both dead and Edmund realizes he was truly loved by them, does he find within himself the compassion necessary to save Cordelia and Lear. As so often during the course of the play, the road to redemption follows the path of love.

Yet how do we justify the appearance of a hanged Cordelia? All the evidence points to an unjust universe ruled by gods who are not concerned with either justice, love or humanity. Therefore, it is extremely difficult to find a moral explanation for Cordelia's death. Only if her death is seen as the punishment for her behavior in Act I Scene 1 does this explanation hold. Otherwise it is difficult to believe that Shakespeare saw the world as a moral one in this play. The only promise of morality comes in Edgar's last words which suggest a world restored to balance and order. But by then all of the central characters except for Kent, who says he is on his way to death, and Albany, who has resigned his leadership, are dead. Only Edgar, the believer in stoical endurance, has survived. Lear, driven mad again by Cordelia's death, voices the central, timeless problem of a seemingly immoral universe: "Why should a dog, a horse, a rat, have life, / And thou no breath at all?" Lear's "poor fool," Cordelia, is dead.

The problems, challenges and questions about *King Lear* have stimulated and intrigued many critics. The play demands that we face our own concept of the world and the nature of the god or gods that inhabit that world. The measure of justice and injustice are still an unknown quantity that each individual must determine finally for themselves. *King Lear* discusses the problems but the solutions the play offers are open-ended and subject to differences in interpretation.

Character Sketches

Lear

Of all Shakespeare's great tragic heroes, Lear is perhaps the least typical. Macbeth is a man of middle age, grizzled and tough in appearance, a man of noble bearing. Hamlet is a young man, fine of feature, noble also in bearing, and often played as a sensitive intellectual. Antony is middle-aged, a man whose very stature speaks of power to the audience, one of the three pillars of the ancient world. But Lear when we first see him is already an old man; his best days have passed, though doubtless there is still about his person a certain regal carriage. He comes on stage with his entourage dressed as king, looking the part of a royal ruler, but almost as soon as he speaks we discover that he is a petulant, almost senile old man.

Lear wears the proper cloak; the outward and visible signs of royalty are clear, but the inward and spiritual graces that make a king are absent. His petulant behavior betrays him, and soon, when he engages his three daughters in the dreadful game of flattery, wherein Goneril and Regan swear the whole allegiance of their hearts to a father, leaving nothing for a husband, it becomes clear that Lear is something less than natural. When Cordelia, the daughter closest to his heart, refuses to engage in the awful process and answers him "nothing," he banishes her. Lear has assumed one of the least attractive roles in Shakespearean literature, that of a bad father.

Already we have enough to force the play quickly to a tragic dimension, although it seems unlikely at the beginning that Lear will be able to arouse either pity or fear in the audience. But Shakespeare soon adds another aspect to his characterization, the Renaissance preoccupation with appearance and reality. Lear is forced to the verge of madness, until it is impossible to tell when he is mad or sane. After the dreadful, moving storm on the heath, Lear seems truly insane, but as we see in the mock trial the line between madness and sanity is a fine one. There is method in his madness. Appearance and reality become intermixed.

At the end of the play Shakespeare restores Lear's sanity and shows him in truly regal light, when he bears the dead Cordelia in his arms. But otherwise Lear lacks greatness almost from the opening scene of the play. At the very end of his life he attains at least a shadow of the regality he might never have lost had he not misjudged others and had he recognized and accepted reality.

High position is an easy way for an author to indicate the stature of a character in a play, but Shakespeare was seldom satisfied with mere formal signs. Often his heroes are capable of great emotions, as Antony is of grand passion, or fine intellectual achievements, as Hamlet comes close to accomplishing. But Lear is never an intellectual, and his great deeds are mingled with madness, as when he runs bare-headed into the storm. Lear is a strange protagonist, but he does arouse our pity as the play progresses and, by some peculiarly Shakespearean magic, our fear and admiration.

Goneril & Regan

The two villains of the play are, as Ridley has claimed, "almost too fiendish to be human." Of the two, Goneril is perhaps more vicious than her younger sister. It is she who suggests gouging out Gloucester's eyes and she who plots her husband's death so that she may fulfill her lust for Edmund. But between them there is really little to choose. Neither has the magnificence of a Lady Macbeth nor the touch of greatness in her villainy that we find in Iago. They represent evil in an elemental form, as Shakespeare suggests it often exists in life. They do not become evil as the play progresses, though we have to discover by watching, horrified, the depth of their degradation. To Lear they are the ever-present symbols of his own folly as well as symbols of wickedness, but to the audience they are evil as it exists in the human soul, a theatrical representation of the curse of Cain or even of original sin.

Kent

Kent has been described as one of Shakespeare's fine "plain, blunt men." As such he belongs to the tradition of Horatio in *Hamlet* or Enobarbus in *Antony & Cleopatra*. He is outspoken, salty, and courageous, but as we have seen just before Cornwall placed him in the stocks, he can flatter, too. Unlike Enobarbus, he is a study in persistent loyalty throughout the play. Kent, too, comes to understand a great deal of the tragic nature of life, but the audience does not often share his exact knowledge. His part is too minor for that.

Cordelia

Cordelia is on stage for very little of the drama. After her appearance in Act I where she refuses to indulge her father in his game of flattery, she disappears until near the end of the play. Her character is never very fully developed, although her presence is constantly felt through the many references Lear makes to her while suffering at the hands of her sisters. Since Cordelia is so sketchy a figure it becomes tempting to see her as a symbol rather than a person. She represents virtue and chastity in a play full of evil and lust. It is possible, however, in even her brief appearances to see a slight change in her behavior. While in Act I she refused to play along with the horrible game of flattery, which after all was a mere formality since Lear was already prepared to give her the largest portion, in the latter part of the play, she begs her father's forgiveness. As well, instead of contradicting her father's vision of their life in prison, she remains silent while he paints a rosy picture of their future. In spite of this subtle change in her character, her presence is felt most strongly in the scenes in which Lear recalls her and in the final scene when he appears bearing her dead body in his arms. As such it seems Shakespeare's intention was not to create a heroine in the tradition of Juliet or Desdemona but rather to create an ideal for the illustration of his themes.

Gloucester

Gloucester's role in the subplot is a parallel to Lear's role in the main plot although Gloucester does not have the tragic grandeur of Lear. In fact Gloucester serves as an illustration of what can happen when a man endures great suffering and does not go mad. Lear's suffering leads him to a sharpened awareness and to madness while Gloucester's trials lead him to a keener perception and despair. He tries to take his own life by jumping off the cliffs of Dover. Later, he begs Edgar to leave him where he stands saying "a man may rot even here." We are to suppose that he eventually learns patience and to accept that the gods determine when we shall live and die. Gloucester's death is effected off-stage so as not to detract our attention and sympathy from the coming tragedies of the deaths of Cordelia and Lear. We are also not permitted to see Gloucester die a noble death because of his somewhat flawed nature. Remember, we are told by him at the beginning of the play that he has been lustful and has fathered an illegitimate son as the consequences. He cannot therefore be a heroic figure but is instead a more ordinary man.

Edgar

Like his father, Edgar serves as a foil to the main plot, but Shakespeare has given him a larger role than Gloucester's. He is also a primary connection between the two plots. At the very end, as the loyal son, he is saved to assume the burdens of state in a kingdom wracked by chaos, a very important role for the future beyond the final scene of the play. But much more interesting is the role he plays throughout the drama, in which, to borrow a phrase from *Hamlet*, he eats the air chameleon-like. In fact Edgar plays more parts and speaks more dialects than any other character in Shakespeare, and the demands placed upon the actor assuming his role are tremendous. At first he is a good, dutiful son, a bit gullible perhaps when he falls into the hands of his brother Edmund, a masterful villain, but when he escapes to the heath he becomes such a powerful pretender of madness that he can challenge Hamlet himself at that game. He later assumes the role of a country rustic, and towards the end of the play we see him again as a noble, though anonymous, knight accepting the challenge that has been hurled against Edmund. Finally, by a process which is an imitation of Lear's, he attains wisdom, and thus he is qualified to serve as regent of Britain.

Edmund

This villain of the Gloucester plot, the traitorous evil son, serves as a kingpin on which the two plots cross and recross each other. As villains go, Edmund is notable, but he is not so important as Iago in *Othello*. At the end of the play Shakespeare makes a feeble attempt to redeem Edmund. He shows us that Edmund's despicable lust for power, for Edgar's inheritance, for the bodies of both evil sisters, is not the real explanation of his disgusting conduct, which includes treachery to his own father. Instead Edmund is at least partly motivated by shame for his status as a bastard. It is not his fault he was not "got 'tween lawful sheets"; this is part of the evil of the world. Thus Shakespeare is more than fair to Edmund when at the last minute, between the stirrup and the ground, as it were, he permits him to perform a redemptive action. He informs Albany's party of the plot he has laid against Lear's and Cordelia's lives and hastens them to the rescue. It is not his fault they are too late. In a Christian milieu such an action might provide some hope for Edmund in the afterlife, but as things stand Shakespeare is not actually claiming any more than that villains, too, like everyone else, are unpredictable. It is up to the audience to draw the conclusion that in the worst of men there may sometimes be a spark of good that awaits kindling.

Cornwall

The Duke of Cornwall, Regan's husband, is the perfect portrait of the public man who has given himself up completely to corruption and courtly intrigue. He gained great place through marriage, never a very good method in Shakespeare, and then gave way to his lusts. Besides, he is stupid. He gets what he deserves, death almost by accident when the servant objecting to his vile treatment of Gloucester somehow manages to wound him. He never understands the depth of his own infamy and serves mostly as a pale foil to his vicious wife.

Albany

The husband of Goneril, Albany, maintains considerable dignity throughout the play. He is the loyal Englishman who has inadvertently fallen among evildoers. At the beginning of the play, he is perhaps too attracted by the gains of policy and too slow-witted to comprehend what is happening, but his instincts are essentially true. As the play progresses, he comes to see Goneril in her true light, even before Edgar gives him her fateful letter to Edmund. When the kingdom is threatened, he struggles with his conscience. Should he support the good cause, which has been taken up by France and thereby become the cause of the invader? Or should he support England and hope to straighten out matters later? It is the latter course he chooses. For a contemporary Elizabethan it was the only realistic solution to this paradox.

The Fool

As the play opens only Kent and Cordelia understand the extent of Lear's folly, but the Fool, whose riddling utterances never fail to delight Shakespearean audiences, soon joins them with a third voice of sanity. Not only is he a wise fool, but, it would seem, he is also undeniably committed to the side of good. Miss Welsford in her book, *The Fool*, frequently refers to him in Christian terms. He is a wise fool to teach a king hastening down the road to madness, but he is not, except verbally, a funny fool. This is no court jester but a voice of inner sanity and outward conscience. The editor Duthie suggests that through him Shakespeare may have wished to remind us of the Psalmist: "Out of the mouths of babes and sucklings hast thou ordained strength because of thine enemies, that thou mightest still the enemy and the avenger."

But we must not consider everything Lear says as mad and everything the Fool says as right. His role is as a tutor to the King. Lear has inverted the natural order of things, permitting his daughters to inherit while he still lives, and the Fool is there to remind him that no good can come of it. After Act III, Scene 6, with the storm raging, the Fool completely disappears from stage never to be seen again. Many critics have suggested reasons for his exit, but of course the main reason is that the Fool is no longer dramatically useful. So long as Lear was on the downgrade, the Fool was needed to remind him of his folly and to plead with him to alter his course. Once the King has reached the bottom of his suffering, the Fool can do nothing for him. He no longer needs to be reminded of his past actions. His way henceforth is through self-knowledge gained at the expense of vast suffering. In that process there is no part for such a Fool.

Minor Characters

The King of France and the Duke of Burgundy

Although only briefly present in the opening scenes, the two wooers for Cordelia's hand do make an impression on us. The Duke of Burgundy, we quickly realize, is interested in self-gain rather than love. The King of France, on the other hand, sees in Cordelia the virtue that Lear ignores. His behavior calls to mind the Christian precepts which declare that in having given up the world there is a better world to be won. He determines to cherish and love the impoverished Cordelia.

Oswald

Oswald is an unlikeable character, supporting Goneril in all her worst endeavors. He carries messages between her and Edmund and acts as a go-between for the armies of Regan and Goneril. His only possibly redeeming quality is loyalty to his mistress. Yet we admire much more the servant who stood up to his master Cornwall in defense of Gloucester than the blind loyalty of Oswald.

The Theme of *King Lear**

King Lear, in spite of its intensity, is a less individual tragedy than is *Othello*. Indeed, although it starts with the family and the innermost circle of human relations, it ranges out through the state and through nature itself to the ultimate and unchangeable aspects of man's life on earth. Lear is at the opposite pole from Hamlet. If a man will not or cannot enter into the solution of his own problem, nature can be counted on to solve it for him. In *King Lear* nature is seen as power, generation, and cohesion. Left alone, it is chaos; subdued and shaped by God's law and man's law, it is order, civilization, justice, and mercy. When Lear gives over his kingdom, he commits a sin against nature and the law of God. Lear's behavior as a father is equally subversive, and throughout the play appear the consequences of the violation of fundamental laws of nature. The stresses and strains of the natural world which Lear has offended finally destroy his sanity, and, as we shall see, the moment can be marked exactly. Thus with the wreck of all ordered systems and the wreck of mind itself *King Lear* becomes perhaps the most far-reaching of all tragedies. It displays the ultimate idea of calamity in the ethics of the Renaissance. In universality *King Lear* rivals *Hamlet*, although the two plays occupy different fields. Hamlet represents the innermost life of all men; Lear, man's life in its social relations.

Dramatically the play is notable for its perfect handling of two plots. Shakespeare had had from the beginning a remarkable power of uniting component plots into unified wholes. Nowhere does he show greater skill than in *King Lear*. For his major plot he went to an anonymous play, a very good one, the old *King Leir*, but seems also characteristically to have read up the Lear story in Geoffrey of Monmouth's *Historia Regum Britonum* and in all available sources. Wilfred Perrett in his *Story of King Lear from Geoffrey of Monmouth to Shakespeare* (Berlin, 1904) makes these facts pretty clear. The most important alteration Shakespeare made in the old plot was to give it a tragic ending, an ending clearly called for in the thought and temper of the Renaissance. The minor plot of Gloucester and his two sons Shakespeare borrowed from Sidney's story of the blind King of Paphlagonia in *Arcadia*. Of the nefarious intrigue between Edmund and the two wicked daughters of Lear and of the belated repentance of the wicked brother there is no trace in Sidney. These features seem brilliantly consequential, and Shakespeare probably invented them. The minor plot itself is an obvious counterpart of the major plot. What then is the major theme of the play?

*Editor's title. From *An Interpretation of Shakespeare*, by Hardin Craig. Columbia: Lucas Brothers, 1948.

King Lear says to Kent, disguised as Caius (Act I, Sc. 4, 28-32),

Dost thou know me, fellow?

And Kent replies,

No, sir, but you have that in your countenance which I
would fain call master.
Lear. What's that?
Kent. Authority.

The underlying concept of *King Lear*, one of those great moral, meaningful themes which Shakespeare often embodies in current thought,
is not ingratitude as many have said. It is authority. *King Lear* is, first
of all, a play about kingship; about a trustful old king, every inch a
king, who in old age brings destruction to himself, and to certain persons in his own circle, and to his country. It is a play which tears off
the outer coverings. Pious and innocent-seeming people who are
villainous, are revealed in their true natures, and the "similar" is
disclosed for what it is, as it works destruction. This is done in a world
in which most men are constantly seeking their own advancement, in a
court in which flatterers are always lurking, and in which a king
should be constantly wary and constantly careful to follow the advice
of such practical honest men as Kent. It is a courtly situation, and
Elizabeth herself has gone down in history as one who did, although
often suspected of heeding flatterers, usually follow the counsels of
the wise. The basis of *King Lear* is belief in authority, in a strong
single rule.

In order to make this theme a tangible thing, or as we say, to give
it artistic embodiment, Shakespeare has used various patterns of
thought, themselves embodied in character, scene, and action, and has
delineated them by these means. There are various structural devices
by the use of which the form of the great concept is rounded out and
completed, voiced and made luminous. The most conspicuous of these
is the plot of Gloucester and his two sons, which parallels closely the
plot of Lear and his three daughters. One may perhaps say that
Gloucester's blinding is symbolic of the destruction of true authority
at the hands of the great social sins of flattery, ambition, sedition, and
usurpation. Ingratitude is King Lear's main plea and it saves him from
the censure which might fall upon him as a consequence of his naked
folly. It is a conventional and expected element in the portrayal of the
suffering, the personal tragedy, of the hero. Ingratitude has somewhat
the same relation to *King Lear* that the motive of fear has to *Macbeth*.

Yet "Monster ingratitude!" and "Ingratitude, . . . marble-hearted
fiend" are less fundamental to the play than are Regan's saying,

he hath ever but slenderly known himself,

and Goneril's reply (Act I, Sc. 1, 296-9),

The best and soundest of his time hath been but rash.

In Renaissance thought, as in ours and in that of the early Greeks, it was important to know oneself, and yet the issue of the play does not turn on the errors of this king. Lear himself defines the issue by suggestion when he protests against the loss of his knights to Goneril and Regan, who have said respectively, "What need you five and twenty, ten, or five?" and "What need one?" (Act II, Sc. 4, 264-86):

O, reason not the need: our basest beggars
Are in the poorest thing superfluous:
Allow not nature more than nature needs,
Man's life's as cheap as beast's: thou art a lady;
If only to go warm were gorgeous,
Why, nature needs not what thou gorgeous wear'st,
Which scarcely keeps thee warm. But, for true need, —

And again, most truly and suggestively, when he says (Act IV, Sc. 6, 97-107):

They flattered me like a dog; and told me I had white hairs in my beard ere the black ones were there. To say 'ay' and 'no' to everything that I said! — 'Ay' and 'no' too was no good divinity. When the rain came to wet me once, and the wind to make me chatter; when the thunder would not peace at my bidding; there I found 'em, there I smelt 'em out. Go to, they are not men o' their words: they told me I was every thing; 'tis a lie, I am not ague-proof.

Kingship in *King Lear* is not conceived of as sovereignty of a political body only, not as an office only, but as a divine institution, the king being the voice of God and the embodiment of God's will. It follows that God installs a king, determines the length of his reign, and makes of loyalty or treason to a king loyalty or treason to God. A king is part of the grand structural unity of the universe, and there is nowhere in Shakespeare such an elaborate use of the microcosmic theory. The whole notion of order and chaos in the universe is involved, and the happenings in this play illustrate the doctrine of Ulysses when he says (*Troilus and Cressida, Act I, Sc. 3,* 108-24):

Take but degree away, untune that string,

And, hark, what discord follows! each thing meets
In mere oppugnancy: the bounded waters
Should lift their bosoms higher than the shores
And make a sop of all this solid globe:
Strength should be lord of imbecility,
And the rude son should strike his father dead:
Force should be right; or rather, right and wrong,
Between whose endless jar justice resides,
Should lose their names, and so should justice too.
Then every thing includes itself in power,
Power into will, will into appetite;
And appetite, an universal wolf,
So doubly seconded with will and power,
Must make perforce an universal prey,
And last eat up himself.

And so the wreck begins. No sooner does King Lear hearken to his flattering daughters than he yields to injustice, injures the frank and innocent Cordelia, and according to the convention observed in *Gorboduc* and everywhere else, banishes the honest courtier Kent. Passion makes him deaf (Act I, Sc. 1, 124-54).

Here starts an under-current in the cosmical structure of this drama which must not remain unobserved, namely, that the ministers of God will ultimately restore the right. Righteous forces are not weaker than those of malignancy but stronger. The suffering of the hero is portrayed in terms of the shifting of grief to anger, righteous anger. Kent stands for the resistance to evil wherever it appears. In Lear there is a long battle between grief and anger, and, when grief wins, insanity results. Gloucester lacks resistance, and the elaborately attempted suicide over the imaginary cliff and many ministrations of his son Edgar are necessary before he accepts salvation in the doctrine (Act V, Sc. 2, 9-11),

Men must endure
Their going hence, even as their coming hither:
Ripeness is all.

Lear never completely weakens (Act IV, Sc. 6, 188-91)

It were a delicate stratagem, to shoe
A troop of horse with felt: I'll put't in proof;
And when I have stolen upon these sons-in-law,
Then, kill, kill, kill, kill, kill, kill!

When Goneril asserts authority over him (Act I, Sc. 4) his indignation blazes out in

The untented woundings of a father's curse.

To read his curses is to understand why curses had validity in Renaissance thought. They are in terms of generic nature, of which Lear is a part (lines 297-311). One passage begins:

Hear, nature, hear; dear goddess, hear!

and ends:

How sharper than a serpent's tooth it is
To have a thankless child!

The first of the natural units to be disrupted is that of the family, the family of Lear and that of Gloucester. In Edmund's attack on Edgar is much of the technique of Iago — hypocrisy, apparent reluctance, delay, opportunism, and the taking advantage of those whose natures are so far from doing harm that they suspect none. There is also use of general and portentous matters to cover up particular chicanery. In one scene (Act V, Sc. 2) there is a conversation, often misunderstood, between Gloucester and Edmund. The religion of *King Lear* is pagan, a sort of nature worship, and it is piety on Gloucester's part for him to say (Act I, Sc. 2, 112-27):

These late eclipses in the sun and moon portend no good to us: though the wisdom of nature can reason it thus and thus, yet nature finds itself scourged by the sequent effects.

He goes on to cite evidence of the disturbance of the natural order, and when he withdraws from the scene, Edmund takes up the theme in a spirit of pure infidelity. Because his rejection of signs and portents is ultra-modern, he has been admired for his realistic stand and has been thought to speak with the voice of Shakespeare. Nothing could be further from the truth; the facts are all against such an opinion, and in the play there is nothing to support it. Gloucester has looked into the future and told us what is about to happen and what does happen. Edmund's words are clever, but they reveal him as a villain and not as a scientist (lines 128-45):

This is the excellent foppery of the world, that, when we are sick in fortune, — often the surfeit of our own behaviour, — we make guilty of our disasters the sun, the moon, and the stars: as if we were villains by necessity; fools by heavenly compulsion; knaves, thieves, and treachers, by spherical predominance; drunkards, liars, and adulterers, by an

enforced obedience of planetary influence; and all that we
are evil in, by a divine thrusting on: an admirable evasion of
whoremaster man, to lay his goatish disposition to the
charge of a star! My father compounded with my mother
under the dragon's tail; and my nativity was under Ursa
major; so that it follows, I am rough and lecherous. Tut, I
should have been that I am, had the maidenliest star in the
firmament twinkled on my bastardizing.

Quite apart from the dramatic situation, it is altogether probable that
Shakespeare, like other Elizabethans, believed that nature acted in
sympathy with man and that event was written in the stars.

The play moves rapidly in the first two acts of *King Lear*. Edgar,
betrayed by Edmund and banished, conceals himself in the disguise of
a Bedlam beggar. Lear makes a stalwart fight broken now and then
with threats of approaching madness, and in the last scene is turned
out into the storm. The first scene of the third act gives news of forces
gathering in France for his succor. There are hints of sedition and civil
war, and we see that the state is suffering disintegration. Then comes
the storm in *King Lear*. It is not improbable to our thinking and must
have been most probable in the thought of Shakespeare that the indif-
ferent elements themselves would at such a time have been mingled as
in primordial chaos. To us it is a tempest of words. The dramatist has
mainly words to serve his turn, and there is nothing quite like this in
literature (Act III, Sc. 2, 1-9):

> Blow, winds, and crack your cheeks! rage! blow!
> You cataracts and hurricanoes, spout
> Till you have drench'd our steeples, drown'd the cocks!
> You sulphurous and thought-executing fires,
> Vaunt-couriers to oak-cleaving thunderbolts,
> Singe my white head! And thou, all-shaking thunder,
> Strike flat the thick rotundity o' the world!
> Crack nature's moulds, all germens spill at once,
> That make ingrateful man!

This aged man has gone to school, and not the least interesting things
to be observed are Lear's own reflections (lines 49-60):

> Let the great gods,
> That keep this dreadful pother o'er our heads,
> Find out their enemies now. Tremble, thou wretch,
> That hast within thee undivulged crimes,
> Unwhipp'd of justice: hide thee, thou bloody hand;
> Thou perjured, and thou simular man of virtue

That art incestuous: caitiff, to pieces shake,
That under covert and convenient seeming
Hast practised on man's life: close pent-up guilts,
Rive your concealing continents, and cry
These dreadful summoners grace. I am a man
More sinn'd against than sinning.

And in scene four (lines 28-36) in a moment of convincing sanity preceding his own mental break-down Lear says,

Poor naked wretches, whereso'er you are,
That bide the pelting of this pitiless storm,
How shall your houseless heads and unfed sides,
Your loop'd and window'd raggedness, defend you
From seasons such as these? O, I have ta'en
Too little care of this! Take physic, pomp;
Expose thyself to feel what wretches feel,
That thou mayst shake the superflux to them,
And show the heavens more just.

But the spectacle of devastation is too much for Lear when he sees the Bedlam beggar. We know it is Edgar in disguise, but to the Elizabethan a man's nature was permeated by a disguise and he became the thing he imitated. When Lear sees him naked and miserable, Edgar becomes a symbol of ultimate destitution, without a trace of what we call civilization, the world that man under the eye of God has built. There is already present the natural imbecile and the Bedlam beggar, and Lear completes the trio by becoming a madman. Perhaps there is no greater climax in Shakespeare (Act III, Sc. 4, 105-40):

Why, thou wert better in thy grave than to answer with thy uncovered body this extremity of the skies. Is man no more than this? Consider him well. Thou owest the worm no silk, the beast no hide, the sheep no wool, the cat no perfume. Ha! here's three on's are sophisticated! Thou art the thing itself: unaccommodated man is no more but such a poor, bare, forked animal as thou art. Off, off, you lendings! come, unbutton here. [*Tearing off his clothes.*]

Thus the ruin of the family, the kingdom, and the natures of men culminates in the ruin of the mind. After this point the theme of ruin appears mainly in the mad talk of Lear in the sixth scene of the fourth act where, in matter and impertinency mixed, is some of the bitterest of pessimism (lines 168-74):

Through tatter'd clothes small vices do appear;

Robes and furr'd gowns hide all. Plate sin with gold,
And the strong lance of justice hurtless breaks;
Arm it in rags, a pigmy's straw does pierce it.
None does offend, none, I say, none; I'll able 'em:
Take that of me, my friend, who have the power
To seal the accuser's lips.

The saner passages appear in a little oasis in Lear's madness created by Gloucester's question, "Is't not the king?" "Ay, every inch a king" is Lear's reply, and as his sanity returns he speaks in blank verse more regular as his thought gains in clarity. One interest of the passage is the expression in detail of the vision of disorder set forth by Ulysses in *Troilus and Cressida* (Act I, Sc. 3, 94-134).

Meantime, in the last scene of the third act, occurs the blinding of Gloucester. Shakespeare had found this horror in Sidney's story of the blind King of Paphlagonia in *Arcadia*. Shakespeare ironically has Gloucester suggest his fate in the words (lines 56-7):

Because I would not see thy cruel nails
Pluck out his poor old eyes.

The event is outrageous, and no glib words about Elizabethan love of violence will justify it. Shakespeare has, however, with his usual tact done something to redeem it. He, long before Ibsen, saw his ordinary people as human beings, so much so that he has been mistakenly called democratic. What he saw was not that all men have an equal right to rule in the state — a later idea — but that even common people are human beings, capable of love, wisdom, bravery, self-sacrifice, and shrewd good sense, each with a feeling of personal pride as true as that of any king or any modern man in a free country. That mere First Servant in *King Lear*, a man without a name, revolts in behalf of humanity. He fights Cornwall and kills him (line 79):

Nay, then, come on, and take the chance of anger.

Not less striking in its recoil to nature is the later history of the old King. How intentionally it was done one does not know, but Shakespeare has given us a picture of Lear restored to sanity, chastened, wise, and at peace with all the world, as serene almost as the king Pippa sings about in *Pippa Passes:*

A King lived long ago,
In the morning of the world,
When earth was nigher heaven than now.

When Lear and Cordelia are captured and carried off he says in idyllic terms (Act V, Sc. 3, 7-21):

> Come, let's away to prison:
> We two alone will sing like birds i' the cage:
> When thou dost ask me blessing, I'll kneel down,
> And ask of thee forgiveness: so we'll live,
> And pray, and sing, and tell old tales, and laugh
> At gilded butterflies, and hear poor rogues
> Talk of court news; and we'll talk with them too,
> Who loses and who wins; who's in, who's out,
> And take upon's the mystery of things,
> As if we were God's spies.

He has arrived at the point where he believes in the existence of love, and love is enough to restore the shattered world.

But rest and peace on earth were not for him. His mighty passion must once more flame through the ages. The quality of that last scene in *King Lear* is suggested by a story told of Edmund Kean. Kean had at last got his opportunity and gained fame as the greatest exponent of human passion who had appeared on the English stage. When his Othello had been proclaimed as a sublime and moving spectacle, he remarked, "The London audience have no idea what I can do until they see me over the dead body of Cordelia."

The staunch old Lear was never more masterly, more practical than at the end of his life (Act V, Sc. 3, 257 ff.):

> She's gone for ever!
> I know when one is dead, and when one lives;
> She's dead as earth. Lend me a looking-glass;
> If that her breath will mist or stain the stone,
> Why, then she lives. . . .
> This feather stirs; she lives! If it be so
> It is a chance which does redeem all sorrows
> That ever I have felt. . . ,
> I might have sav'd her; now she's gone forever!
> Cordelia, Cordelia! stay a little. Ha!
> What is't thou say'st? Her voice was ever soft,
> Gentle, and low; an excellent thing in woman.
> I kill'd the slave that was a-hanging thee.
> *Capt.* 'Tis true, my lords, he did.
> *Lear.* Did I not, fellow?
> I have seen the day, with my good biting falchion
> I would have made them skip.

It was Lamb who said "the Lear of Shakespeare cannot be acted."

That is true to this extent, that it requires a genius to do the part full justice. There is much that is disappointing in the early Lear. He is so wise, so observant, so experienced that he ought not, for example, to have failed to see the difference between Cordelia and his other daughters. Being the man he is, he should have seen that Cordelia was ashamed to display her tenderness before the world and too proud to buy a dowry with it. Lear's mind and heart must have been asleep, perhaps partly never awakened, until fate issued its writ and put him on trial. Thus an old story of kingship becomes a play about kingship, although the suffering of Lear, embodying much of the poetry, learning, and humanity of Shakespeare, at times overshadows everything else. It was not only a Renaissance characteristic, but particularly a characteristic of Shakespeare, to look beyond the sufferings of men and endeavor to discover the larger forces at work as causes and concomitants. By this means emotional strength and artistic validity are established.

Lear is thus the tragedy not of a single individual, but of society, Lear being the symbol as well as the chief protagonist. As might be expected in the treatment of such a theme, all the participants are fully realized. Lear in his troubles is not without supporters and advocates — men of justice, courage, and wisdom. The honest, loyal, and intelligent Kent has been the theme of much praise. His humor, his realism, his vigorous action are irresistible. His philosophical acceptance of the stocks, his natural antipathy to Oswald the sycophant, and his persistent care of Lear seem crowned in his great speech (Act V, Sc. 3, 313-15):

> Vex not his ghost: O, let him pass! he hates him much
> That would upon the rack of this tough world
> Stretch him out longer.

Edgar is something of a hero of romance, and has in him some flavor of *Arcadia*; and, if one must see virtue in the miserable Restoration version of *King Lear*, which gave the play a happy ending, one might say that Tate did well in marrying Cordelia off to Edgar. He is a clever, resourceful man of tender heart. It was he who saved old Gloucester's soul with the elaborate counterfeiting of suicide, and, in that connection, we owe to Edgar, whose motives were purely filial, one of the most perfect bits of descriptive literature in the language (Act IV, Sc. 6, 11-24):

> How fearful
> And dizzy 'tis, to cast one's eyes so low!
> The crows and choughs that wing the midway air
> Show scarce so gross as beetles: half way down

Hangs one that gathers samphire, dreadful trade!
Methinks he seems no bigger than his head:
The fishermen, that walk upon the beach,
Appear like mice; and yond tall anchoring bark,
Diminish'd to her cock; her cock, a buoy
Almost too small for sight: the murmuring surge,
That on the unnumbered idle pebbles chafes,
Cannot be heard so high. I'll look no more;
Lest my brain turn, and the deficient sight
Topple down headlong.

And it is Edgar who utters the thought, congenial to Shakespeare and the Renaissance, which sums up the lesson poor Gloucester has learned (Act V, Sc. 2, 9-11):

Men must endure
Their going hence, even as their coming hither:
Ripeness is all.

In this play old men are put to school, and the pathos of Gloucester, less obvious, is deeper than that of Lear. It is his pity for Lear that brings upon him his calamity and later affords a means by which Edgar may rescue him body and soul.

Edmund is a striking character, a man who, like Iago and Richard III, chooses villainy as his part. He is the most varied and perhaps the most interesting of Shakespeare's studies of evil men. Edmund is a bastard and, according to current belief, is born outside the framework of social and moral conformity. He shows great intelligence in making his way, and, although abominable in his actions, he is not at bottom devoid of humanity. There is something open and brilliant about his downfall; he is neither dour, silent, and obdurate like Iago nor swept away in a tempest of passion like Richard and Macbeth. He confesses and, to some degree, repents, saying significantly (Act V, Sc. 3, 243-4):

I pant for life: some good I mean to do
Despite of mine own nature.

It is in conformity with Edmund's nature and situation that he should find the stepping-stones of his rise to power in unsanctioned relations with the unnatural women who have wronged their father. The passion that they both entertain for him brings a threefold destruction in its wake, since it is the inciting force for Goneril's murder of Regan, Goneril's suicide, and Edmund's destruction in combat. The roles of the two wicked sisters are parallel, and it is not easy to discriminate between them. Dowden calls Goneril "the calm wielder of a pitiless force, the resolute initiator of cruelty," who knows that a helpless old man is merely a helpless old man and that words are only words. Dowden thinks Regan "more unmeasured in her ferocity" and "a smaller, shriller, fiercer, more eager piece of malice."

Cordelia is undoubtedly one of the finer women in Shakespeare's gallery of portraits. The tests with which she is confronted are masculine. She is too honorable to flatter or to lie or to remain silent in the presence of dishonesty. She goes forth to France unsupported and there bends her efforts to the attack on evil. Perhaps Shakespeare could not permit a French army to make conquests in England, or, more probably, he borrowed from the sources the story of her later defeat at the hands of her rebellious nephews; but, in any case, Cordelia suffers defeat. It is on her return to England that Shakespeare makes his perfect depiction of womanly tenderness. The scene of Lear's restoration to sanity (Act IV, Sc. 7) and of the capture (Act V, Sc. 3) are great in their revelation of Cordelia's noble spirit. Her one remark in the latter scene seems to characterize her to perfection and to set her apart from other women in the plays (lines 3-6):

> We are not the first
> Who, with best meaning, have incurr'd the worst,
> For thee, oppressed king, am I cast down;
> Myself could else out-frown false fortune's frown.

The Fool has puzzled the world, as simplicity, innocence, and helplessness will always puzzle it. He illuminates all the earlier part of the play with that wisdom which issues from the mouths of babes and sucklings. After the sixth scene of the third act he strangely disappears. What, if any, exigencies of casting characters may have caused this we do not know.

Imagery in *King Lear**

An attempt to interpret a Shakespearian play solely on the basis of its imagery — a risky undertaking — would have the greatest chance of success if *King Lear* were the play in question. The imagery here seems to be more fully integrated into the structure of the drama and for that reason to play a more meaningful rôle than in other plays. Not only do the various sequences of imagery offer important clues to what Shakespeare sought to represent in *King Lear*, but the distribution of the images among the characters, their interrelation and their significance for the illumination of certain themes and trends of the action also help us to a better insight into the meaning of the drama. In *King Lear*, action and imagery appear to be particularly closely dependent upon each other and are reciprocally illuminating; the imagery, in fact, seems to have taken over some functions which so far — in Shakespeare's earlier plays — belonged to other mediums of dramatic expression. In the development of Shakespeare's imagery, *King Lear* therefore represents an important new stage. . . . At the very first glance we perceive that the form of most of the images and their connection with the context differ from those in the earlier plays. Formerly, the images were used as illustrations, or the metaphorical element was fused with the train of thought as a means of enhancement or elucidation. In *King Lear* we can seldom speak of such an illustrative function. The image is presented as if it existed for its own sake: it serves no other aim but to speak for itself alone. Let us look at Lear's speeches in Act III, Scene 2 or in Act IV, Scene 6 from this point of view: he sets image after image as independent, direct visions. The same thing holds true of the Fool. Up to now, we have found characters speaking exclusively in imagery only in moments of the greatest excitement. In *King Lear*, however, this is the case throughout many scenes; imagery is for Lear his most characteristic form of utterance.

The reason for this becomes clear if we trace Lear's development during the early scenes. The first shows us Lear still in possession of his power; he is still a member of society. He makes decisions, gives orders and makes plans, addresses the other characters of this scene, his daughters, Kent, France, etc. But the very first scene gives us a hint of how Lear is going to lose contact with this natural relation to his environment. The dialogue which he carries on with his daughters is at bottom no true dialogue, that is, a dialogue based on a mutual will to mutual understanding.

*Editor's Title. From *The Development of Shakespeare's Imagery*, by W. H. Clemen. Cambridge, Mass.: Harvard University Press, 1951.

Lear determines in advance the answers he will receive: he fails to adapt himself to the person with whom he is speaking. Hence his complete and almost incomprehensible misunderstanding of Cordelia. Lear takes no pains to understand what Cordelia is really trying to say: he does not consider whether her words could not have quite another meaning. He catches up only their superficial form and, because he had expected another answer, different from this, he repels the one person who in reality is nearest and dearest to him. More and more Lear loses contact with the outside world; words become for him less a means of communication with others than a means of expressing what goes on within himself. His utterances, even when addressed to other persons, take on, increasingly, the character of a monologue and become less and less part of the dramatic dialogue, although Lear (which is typical) never speaks an actual monologue himself.

The wealth of images in his speech results from this process and gives it expression; we have seen that in Shakespeare, the monologue is always the form of utterance richest in imagery. Lear gazes within himself; he no longer sees people nor what goes on about him. In madness a man is alone with himself; he speaks more to his own person than to others; where he does not speak to himself, he creates for himself a new and imaginary partner. Lear speaks to people not present, he speaks to the elements, to nature, to the heavens. Men have forsaken him; so he turns to the non-human, superhuman powers. It is one of the functions of the imagery in *King Lear* to awaken these elemental forces and to open to them the way into the play.

The characters around Lear, too, the Fool, Edgar and Kent, speak a language rich in imagery. We shall discuss later the significance of the image in their utterances. If we glance, however, at the other group of characters, Edmund, Goneril, Regan, Cornwall, we note how seldom they employ images, how different is their whole language. In contrast to Lear and his followers, we never find that peculiar form of "monologic dialogue" between them. They speak rationally; they address their words to their partner, and converse in a deliberate and conscious manner. They have a goal which they seek to attain and everything they have to say is bent upon this. Their language does not betray to us what is taking place within them — in the form of "imaginative visions"; it reveals to us solely their aims and attitudes, and how they intend to put these into practice. Thus their language scarcely changes throughout the course of the play, whereas Lear's, Edgar's and Kent's way of speaking is constantly varied. Goneril, Regan and Edmund are the calculating, cool and unimaginative people who are incapable of "creative" imagery. They have no relationship to nature, to the elemental powers. Their world is the world of reason; they live and speak within the narrow limits of their plans, within the limits drawn by the plot and the given moment of the action. Lear's language continually points beyond these limits. Thus the distribution of the images among the characters also gives us a hint as to their position within the play.

The middle acts of the tragedy, Acts II-IV, are the richest in imagery. The outer action is less important here and is relegated to the background. The main emphasis does not fall upon the outer course of events, upon what Regan or Goneril are planning, or what Edmund is about, but rather upon what is passing in Lear himself. The outer drama has become an inner drama. Beneath the surface of the plot lies the deeper level of inner experience which gradually frees itself more and more from the sparse events of the action. The latter becomes a frame and an occasion in order that the former may take on living reality. In truth, Shakespeare has not treated this outer action with the same thoroughness and care as he usually employed in the construction of the plot. As Bradley has already pointed out, the plot displays a number of inconsistencies and is not carried out clearly.Goethe found the action of *Lear* full of improbabilities, and "absurd." But Shakespeare was concerned not with the "outer," but with the "inner" drama. The important thing is not what Lear does, but what he suffers, feels and envisions with his inner eye. One of the greatest and deepest truths of this play is that we must first go through suffering before we can recognize our real selves and the truth. "I stumbled when I saw," Gloucester cries out (Act IV, Sc. 1); he first learned to see, when he was blind. Thus Lear, too, sees through the world of appearances not with his physical eyes; it is rather with his inner eye — in madness — that he penetrates to the very bottom of things and recognizes their true nature, whereas he formerly let himself be blinded by their outward appearance. It is obvious that imagery is the only adequate form of expression for such an inner process.

But the term "inner drama" is not sufficient to describe accurately the peculiar shifting of emphasis — from the level of human action to another level. Much of what Lear utters in the central scenes points beyond the limits of his personal fate. Indeed, Lear's suffering and experience, although represented to us as an individual case, is meant to signify much more than something merely personal; it is meant to be an archetype of the universal. More than in any other play, the human events in *King Lear* are related to the happenings of the whole world. Bradley speaks of the "feeling which haunts us in *King Lear*, as though we were witnessing something universal — a conflict not so much of particular persons as of the powers of good and evil in the world." Behind Lear's personal suffering stands the suffering of the whole world; behind the severing of the bond between Lear and his daughters stands the breakdown of all the hard-and-fast limits of the universe. This inclusive action is made clear to us by means of the imagery. The imagery gives the horizon of the individual occurrence a comprehensive perspective; it transforms human matters into mighty universal events. The elemental forces and the things of nature, as they appear so profusely in the language of Lear and his followers from the second act on, often seem to grow beyond the speakers. They assume, as it were, an individual existence, they become almost independent of the speakers. The imagery becomes the means by which these forces of nature enter into the play and take part therein as active agents. These sequences of imagery, such as are to be found, for example, in Edgar's long list of animals and plants, are not to be interpreted as the "expression" of individual inner experiences, but rather as the appearance of independent forces which belong to the play just as much as to the people. The words "atmosphere," "background," no longer suffice to designate what of nature, landscape and animal world is evoked by the imagery. This "atmosphere" here becomes a world in itself; we almost forget that it is only through the words of certain characters that life is given to this world of nature.

The non-human nature-world enters into the play in the same measure as the human world breaks down and falls to pieces. This occurs when the father is expelled by his daughters, when the son is persecuted by the father and madness dissolves human order; the firm bonds and laws of human society are destroyed; so now non-human powers, heavenly forces, lightning, thunder, rain and wind, animals and plants, enter in rich variety. This interrelationship is to be seen clearly in the structure of the play; the first act contains relatively little nature-imagery; in the second act it begins to grow, and it attains to its height in the third and fourth acts, which show us the forsaken Lear in his madness.

In the first scene of the play we may study the peculiar nature of "dramatic imagery," consisting in preparing for later issues and giving hints of the further development of the action. For the reasons explained above, the first scene is relatively poor in images; but where they do occur, their appearance is significant.

When Lear appears for the first time upon the stage and communicates to the assembled court and to his daughters his intention to divide the kingdom, he says:

> And 'tis our fast intent
> To shake all cares and business from our age,
> Conferring them on younger strengths while we
> Unburdened *crawl* toward death.   (Act I, Sc.1, 39-42)

crawl awakens a definite notion. Taken from the realm of animal life, crawling suggests a wounded, tired, perhaps hunted animal dragging itself nearer to death. Lear, at this point still in full possession of his royal authority, employs the metaphor ironically; he has as yet no knowledge of the fate which will actually cast him out and bring him down to the level of the animals.

We find the next metaphorical passage of this scene when Lear irrevocably disinherits Cordelia:

> Let it be so. Thy truth then be thy dower. . . .
> Here I disclaim all my paternal care, . . .
>   (Act I, Sc. 1, 110-15)

Lear's security is shaken for the first time by Cordelia's misunderstood renouncement. It is no mere chance that Lear at just this moment should turn to the non-human powers, call upon them and repudiate his fathership in their name. This reveals his relationship to the elemental powers: it is awakened when his relationship to the human world is shaken, and it is intensified, as if by a law of nature, by every further wound and repulse he receives from this quarter. On this first occasion we have not yet the form of the direct apostrophe, but the formula of the oath. When Goneril — some scenes later — expels him, Lear again turns to those powers of the underworld. We have a preparatory abrupt flash in "Darkness and devils! Saddle my horses" (Act I, Sc. 4, 273-74), and a few lines later, the first great explosion of this feeling in the apostrophe to nature (line 297). When Goneril reappears, we hear: "Blast and fogs upon thee," and when finally his other daughter also rejects him, the elemental forces are called upon once again:

> You nimble lightnings, dart your blinding flames
> Into her scornful eyes. Infect her beauty,
> You fen-sucked fogs, drawn by the powerful sun
> To fall and blast her pride.   (Act II, Sc. 4,167-70)

The great apostrophes to the elements in the heath scene are the culmination of this sequence; we shall discuss them later. Thus light is thrown from these later passages upon the passage in the first scene.

When Kent in the first scene repeatedly takes the part of the unjustly treated Cordelia, Lear answers impatiently:

> The bow is bent and drawn, make from the shaft.
> *Kent.* Let it fall rather, though the fork invade
> The region of my heart.   (Act I, Sc. 1, 145-47)

This is the first independent image of the scene; the more excited Lear becomes, the more often do images appear in his language. The form of the comparison, such as we still have in the simile of the barbarous Scythian (Act I, Sc. 1, 118), is soon replaced by more direct and forceful metaphorical language in "Come not between the dragon and his wrath" (Act I, Sc. 1, 124). By the well-known image of the bent bow Lear seeks to warn Kent of continuing in his contradiction; twenty lines later he seizes the sword. But beyond the significance of the moment, this image simultaneously contains dramatic irony: with the transfer of the crown to his daughters Lear has surrendered his own position and power; at this moment, without being aware of it, he has delivered himself up to his coming fate. Nothing can now recall the arrow.

When Lear threatens Kent with the sword, Kent replies:

> Kill thy physician, and the fee bestow
> Upon the foul disease.   (Act I, Sc. 1, 166-67)

This designation as physician is also premonitory, for the title comes to full realization only in Kent's rôle in the last acts. "The foul disease," too, is forewarning; it points to the ungrateful daughters and to what they are later to signify for Lear's own feelings. Here, in this first scene, Kent is the only one who has a presentiment of this; but soon, in the second act, Lear himself will say to Goneril:

> But yet thou art my flesh, my blood, my daughter,
> Or rather a *disease* that's in my flesh
> Which I must needs call mine. Thou art a boil,
> A plague sore, an embossed carbuncle,
> In my corrupted blood. (Act II, Sc. 4, 224-28)

A final example may serve to show how here, at the beginning of the play, short metaphors and hints suggest what is more fully unfolded by the imagery of the later scenes. France, the future husband of Cordelia, uses the following words in speaking to Lear of Cordelia:

> Sure, her offense
> Must be of such unnatural degree
> That monsters it, or your forevouched affection
> Fall'n into taint. (Act I, Sc. 1, 221-24)

France employs the metaphor "monsters" in regard to Cordelia's alleged attitude, wherein lies a reproach against Lear, but at the same time dramatic irony as well. For in the course of the play the word "monster" will have its specific application to the ingratitude and the inhuman behaviour of the two other daughters.

Thus many images in this first scene are prophetic. What Herder, speaking more generally, said of the first scene also applies to the imagery: "Lear . . . in the very first scene of his appearance on the stage already bears within himself all the seeds of his destinies for the harvest of the darkest future."

The figure in the play for whom the image is an even more characteristic form of expression than for Lear, is that of the Fool. The Fool never speaks in blank verse, indeed he never comes near the more conventional, measured and dignified manner of speech such as we find, for example, in the first part of the first scene. From the very beginning he has his own peculiar way of expressing himself, a manner which marks him as an outsider. In the speech of the Fool, Shakespeare has given the images wholly new functions. But what is the significance of the image in his case?

We have already stated that in the very first scene Lear loses the capacity for really understanding others in conversation; he cannot carry on a real dialogue. The words of the others no longer reach him or, if they do, in an ill-conveyed meaning. Lear shuts himself off; he becomes isolated in his speech, which from now on, even in the dialogue, bears the stamp of a monologue. The usual manner of speech can therefore no longer move him; such words can neither help nor heal Lear who, in his madness, needs help more and more. The Fool knows this from the very beginning, and he speaks to the King in simile, proverb and image and in rhymed adages and sayings which have the same purpose as his images. Much of what the Fool says Lear neither hears nor grasps, for much is indeed spoken more to the audience than to the King. But part comes home to him and this he does comprehend. Even if Lear replies to only a few of the Fool's utterances, that is still no proof of what Lear may really have heard and understood. For much of the Fool's talk expects no answer. He inserts his sayings and comparisons between the speeches of the others, and he sings his little songs as an outsider, as it were — in this respect his position is often similar to the chorus of the classical tragedy — and formulates most of what he says not as if it were coined to fit a particular case, or were directed at a particular person. "He that hath ears to hear let him hear!" It is the image which makes this unobtrusive parenthetical way of speaking possible. The image clothes the individual and particular case in a more general form; it may take away the sting. Between Lear and the Fool a new form of the dialogue develops which is no longer based upon rational communication, upon the simple play of question and answer, but which is a finer and more subtle interplay of shifting meanings and hints.

The more Lear becomes a victim of self-delusion and madness, the more it becomes the task of the Fool to express in epigrammatic images the unreality of Lear's behaviour, his self-deception and his error. The images of the Fool are the dry and almost trivial language of reality which is continually contrasted with Lear's separation from the outside world. In the great scenes on the heath Lear reaches heights of fantasy and emotion which far transcend human proportions; he becomes a gigantic superhuman figure whose huge dimensions threaten to overstep the limits of what may be represented upon the stage and within the scope of a drama. Here the Fool has the continual function "to keep the scene in touch with reality" (Granville-Barker). For no matter how tremendously the horizon spread out before us in these scenes may widen, the presentation of the play never loses itself in a sphere of the fantastically unreal. Lear himself, as Granville-Barker has shown, returns again and again to intimate, earthly things, he again and again resorts to simplicity and actuality. But it is especially the little sayings and similes of the Fool pertaining to the triviality of every day which counterbalance the gigantic dimensions of Lear's feelings and ideas. The Fool understands how to reduce Lear's behaviour to the simplest, most uncomplicated images of actuality, so that the state of affairs becomes perfectly obvious. Thus, for example, by means of the trivial simile of the egg which Lear has divided to give away both halves (the two crowns) he shows how simple is the division of the kingdom and the relinquishment of the royal power (Act I, Sc. 4, 173). In spite of this simplicity, the Fool's images may have a complex meaning and may give us hints of things still hidden. This passage, thirty lines later, harks back to the image just mentioned: "thou hast pared thy wit o'both sides and left nothing i' the middle. Here comes one o' the parings" (Act I,

Sc. 4, 206). The voluntary dispossession of property is seen as a relinquishing of reason. The ceding of both halves of the land without leaving anything for himself was like the paring of reason on both sides without leaving anything in the middle — so blind and foolish. Thus the rapid transition to "paring" becomes comprehensible; Goneril represents the half of the kingdom given away and at the same time, through her, Lear will go mad. Thus many of the Fool's other images serve to light up the situation with a single flash and, furthermore, to draw the obvious conclusion and to clothe in the universally intelligible language of the proverb what the language of the action is unable to epitomize so convincingly (cf. Act I, Sc. 4, 124; Act I, Sc. 5, 8; Act I, Sc. 5, 30; Act II, Sc. 4, 7; Act II, Sc. 4, 68; Act III, Sc. 6, 13).

At first glance, the images of the Fool, gathered as they are from the unexciting sphere of everyday common sense and often expressing trivial commonplaces, seem to stand in contrast to the great issues of the Lear drama. Fateful predestinations, even aberrations of such tragic weight and such great pathos — thus we could argue — may not be viewed from a merely utilitarian or common-sense standpoint. But it is precisely these simple, uncomplicated conclusions which form the path by which Lear and we, the audience, are led to a deeper and more moving recognition of the ultimate truth.

The effect of image, rhymed proverb and maxim is different from the effect of the direct admonition. Images as well as proverbs can convey a meaning in a manner more impersonal and universally valid. Images, as they are employed by the Fool, free the action from the narrow restrictions of the moment — they assist in producing a detached attitude of mind. The little songs which the Fool sings, further enhance this quieting effect which liberates us and creates this detachment: "the greater the force of the truth, the lighter, the calmer and the more detached appears the form." The songs of the Fool as well as his images indicate a relaxation and a diminution of the suspense in the structure of the scenes — this being, indeed, to a large degree the function of the Fool. If we recall to mind the early Elizabethan tragedies, the *Spanish Tragedy or Titus Andronicus*, we see that such relaxation and counterbalancing are there entirely wanting: everything moves in extremes, every gesture, every word, every action is aimed at achieving the highest possible degree of glaring and bloody effect. In the later Elizabethan drama the Fool with his songs belongs, of course, to the conventions. But nowhere else are he and his forms of utterance employed in so profound a manner, at one and the same time creating detachment and pointing beyond the immediate issue, as here in *King Lear*. . . .

Lear's inner development is portrayed in images more than that of any other character in Shakespeare. The great apostrophes to the elemental forces of nature in the scenes on the heath have already revealed a significant change in Lear. The images of the next scenes, in which the

King goes mad, are again illuminating for Lear's state of mind. The swiftly passing images, logically unconnected with each other, which we hear Lear utter, correspond to the abnormal mental state of the King; they are the adequate form of perception and expression of a lunatic. "It is his mind which is laid bare," Charles Lamb said as an interpretation of these strange speeches — especially in the fourth act. Lear's insanity should not be dismissed as simple craziness. It is rather another manner of perception, by means of which, however, Lear now sees and recognizes what formerly remained concealed to him, as long as he was sane. These images are the fragments of his inner visions, which have not yet attained to the form of thoughts; they have not yet been transformed, ordered and connected in logical sequence and in the service of clear statement. Many images in the fourth act become more comprehensible if light is thrown upon them from previous passages. In the great scene on the heath we hear Lear cry out:

> Let the great gods, . . .
> That art incestuous.   (Act III, Sc. 2, 49-55)

The sins of earth pass before Lear's inner eye as visionary images — the thanklessness of his daughters brings him to the thanklessness and unrighteousness of the whole world. At first judge of his daughters (cf. the judgement scene played in madness with the Fool and Kent, Act III, Sc. 6), Lear becomes in the fourth act the judge of all creatures. From the passage quoted above there runs a connecting link to Act IV, Scene 6, 163-65.

> Thou rascal beadle, hold thy bloody hand!
> Why dost thou lash that whore? Strip thine own back.

Lear, having experienced in his personal world the destruction of human right and order, thus gains insight into the common injustice and frailty of all mankind. His fancy now sees examples of this everywhere in the world. License appears to him in the form of animal-images (Act IV, Sc. 6, 114) and in the vision of the "simpering dame" (line 120); injustice and mendacity in the image of the railing judge (line 155), of the beggar running from the farmer's dog (line 159), of the hypocritical beadle, and of the magnificent robes which cover vice (line 169). In madness Lear has won eyes for reality. His inner eye pierces the outer appearance and penetrates to the true nature of things.

Lear's recovery in the fifth act, too, is clearly reflected in the imagery. Peaceful and delicate things have taken the place of the unclean and repulsive images, and his language is connected, musical and gentle:

> We two alone will sing like birds i' the cage.
> When thou dost ask me blessing, I'll kneel down
> And ask of thee forgiveness. So we'll live,
> And pray, and sing, and tell old tales, and laugh
> At gilded butterflies, . . .   (Act V, Sc. 3, 9-13)

This mood, however, is again interrupted by the terrible and painful experience of Cordelia's death. The fourfold "Howl" when Lear "re-enters with Cordelia dead in his arms" recalls the animal-imagery, and in the next lines spoken by Lear the gigantic and powerful nature of Lear is once again given expression through imagery:

> Had I your tongues and eyes, I'd use them so
> That heaven's vault should crack.   (Act V, Sc. 3, 258-59)

Lear translates all feelings into bodily terms. His imagery thus conveys to us the impression of immense physical force or, if mental suffering is to be expressed, of immense physical pain. The imagery thus helps to intensify and sharpen the poignancy of the spiritual experience through which Lear has to pass. The above image is the last link in a chain which runs through the whole drama.

The Sight Pattern of Imagery in *King Lear**

Gloucester's blindness is by no means a chance product of bitter vengefulness, interchangeable with any other punitive mutilation that might have satisfied his tormentors. Like that of Oedipus, it is wholly in harmony with the aesthetic and moral context; it is the center of a whole family of cross references. Its ironic relationship to Gloucester's own defect of insight is clear enough. But that relationship is not merely left to inference; it is carefully established by the sight pattern, which not only tells us a good deal about Gloucester but is used to help qualify all the main characters in the play.

Gloucester's tragic flaw is a special kind of lack of insight. Gloucester is not a stupid man, but he is a man who does not ask enough questions, who takes evidence at its face value, who confounds appearance and substance. He is the man of the world, the sophisticate, as we might say, who has the naiveté ironically inseparable from the type. His whole history is consistent. Long before the time of the play he enjoyed an adulterous liaison of which Edmund was the fruit — a liaison which indicated that he viewed sex morality entirely as a man of the world. His unperceptive worldliness is the opening note of the play: in the first few lines he talks to Kent with jaunty wit about his escapade with Edmund's mother — even, it appears, within earshot of Edmund. Gloucester does not take the trouble to go beneath the surface, he falls in with whatever is going on about him: this is his way of avoiding responsibility. When Edmund makes a specious case against Edgar (Act I, Sc. 2), Gloucester falls right in with Edmund's plans; he shows what we come to recognize as his characteristic suggestibility, and he dodges the responsibility of finding out what lies behind the superficial evidence. Lear's strange conduct and what he

*Editor's title. From "I Stumbled When I Saw", by Robert B. Heilman, in *This Great Stage: Image and Structure in "King Lear"*. Baton Rouge: Louisiana State University Press, 1948.

supposes to be that of Edgar elicit from him little more than startled exclamations; he wants to charge these distresses up to the "late eclipses in the sun and moon" (Act I, Sc. 2, 112) — a convenient way of evading moral inquiry (very significantly, this astrological habit of mind is shared by no one else in the play). *Eclipses*, at the same time, is one of the hints of the *darkness* in which the now sound-eyed Gloucester is regularly operating. The light in which he sees things lights up only the surface of the world. It is quite consistent that he is inclined to get on with the new political regime: he plainly has his doubts about the way in which things are going, but that a principle is involved, a principle on which he should take a stand, simply does not occur to him. He falls in again. He regrets Cornwall's stocking Lear's follower, Kent (Act II, Sc. 2, 147ff.); but he himself contributes to the infuriation of Lear by his efforts to "fix it up" between him and Cornwall. "You know the fiery quality of the Duke," he tells Lear (Act II, Sc.4, 93), and, more maddeningly for Lear, "I would have all well betwixt you" (line 121). Gloucester hopes that he can "do business with" Cornwall; despite his genuine discomfort, he inclines toward the status quo. The *de facto*, the immediate, the circumscribing world hypnotize him: he cannot question. Yet Gloucester is not unalterably a band-wagon man; he can rise to become a tragic figure, and finally, shocked into a new alertness, he undertakes the commitment to Lear which is his ruin in the practical world whose creature he has been, but at the same time the salvation of his soul. But his spiritual awakening is very subtly managed; there is a fine stroke in the ambiguity of the terms in which Gloucester tells Edmund that he intends to aid Lear (Act III, Sc. 3). There is no doubt whatever that he pities Lear and realizes — note his phrase, "this unnatural dealing" (lines 1-2) — at last that more is involved than political bad taste. But it is also true that he has been abused and mistreated by the usurpers, and that he says, "These injuries the King now bears will be revenged home; there's part of a power already footed; we must incline to the King" (Act III, Sc. 3, 12-14). He is waking up to the moral state of affairs, but in his consciousness there is also some hint that to be pro-Lear may be a good thing; and he is at least in part maneuvering toward the comfortable stream of history. Gloucester does not consciously seek evil, or deliberately hunt for feather beds; it is simply that he is tragically slow in seeing what is implied in the situations in which he finds himself.

His being blinded, then, is an ironic completion of his career (Act III, Sc. 7). The symbolic reverberations of the scene are virtually unmistakable; yet Shakespeare does not leave the perception of them to chance. In fact, almost as if intent upon making us see them, Shakespeare continues with this material which is fresh in our minds and devotes the very next scene (Act IV, Sc. 1) to Gloucester. When the Old Man says, "You cannot see your way" (Act IV, Sc. 1, 19), Gloucester replies:

I have no way and therefore want no eyes.

> I stumbled when I saw.   (lines 20-21)

Thus the symbolism becomes explicit: Gloucester here summarizes his whole career. With eyes he did not see, but now, blind, he has come a long way — far enough even to see into himself. He is beginning to master the eternal human problem. And he goes on:

>   Ah, dear Son Edgar, . . .
> Might I but live to see thee in my touch,
> I'd say I had eyes again!   (lines 23-26)

Though he can now only touch Edgar, he *sees* him — that is, the truth about him — as he did not see him before. And seeing Edgar is itself a symbol of understanding, so that, if Edgar were again restored to him, he could feel that he had eyes — that is, the power for which eyes are a symbol. Thus all the evidence of drama and language points to the conclusion that Gloucester's *hamartia* is, as we have said, failure to see essential things. Furthermore, it seems clear, this failure is meant to be evidenced in the original adultery which Coleridge regards as Gloucester's originating moral misdeed. Near the end the philosophical Edgar, speaking of Gloucester, says to Edmund, "The dark and vicious place where thee he got/Cost him his eyes" (Act V, Sc. 3, 172-73). A reader sensitive to the symbolic pattern can hardly read *dark* as a mere rhetorical flourish or didactic cliché, especially when it is juxtaposed with "Cost him his eyes"; the place was *dark* because years before, Gloucester was exhibiting a characteristic failure to see what his deed involved. The unity of his career as it is symbolized in the sight pattern, is further supported by the bitter lines of Gloucester near the end of the scene quoted above (Act IV, Sc. 1), when he is making his arrangements to be guided by "Tom":

> Let the superfluous and lust-dieted man,
> That slaves your ordinance, that will not see
> Because he doth not feel, feel your power quickly.
>   (lines 70-72)

At first glance we may take Gloucester's word to be an invoking of divine wrath against common types of evildoer. Actually, however, Gloucester is describing himself: he was "lust-dieted" and he "slaved" (i.e., condemned) divine ordinance; he would not see because he did not feel; and he has now felt — the repetition of the verb points to his sharpened sensibility — divine power. He understands himself wholly: the blind man has come to insight.

The irony of Gloucester's final condition is exactly paralleled by the irony of his earlier actions as a man with good eyes. Just when he most fails to see where he is going, he feels, like Oedipus, most shrewd and observant. The sight pattern points the issues for us. While he is being made to see things as Edmund wishes, Gloucester feels that he is detecting the truth: "Let's see," he demands of Edmund three times (Act I, Sc. 2, 35-44) — and he does not see. Again, " . . . if it be nothing, I shall not need spectacles" (line 36). Spectacles are a symbol of what he does need: Shakespeare hits upon the characteristic human frailty by which the denial of a deficiency actually announces the deficiency. It is altogether logical, then, that Edmund's next move against Edgar takes place *at night* (Act II, Sc. 1): the physical darkness betokens Gloucester's failure to see into what is going on. The actors in the nocturnal setting, indeed, represent more than one phase of a human plight: Gloucester victimizes and Edgar is victimized — he flees at night — because of the same kind of unseeingness. It is a meaningful, not merely a rhetorical, irony when Edmund calls, "Light, ho, here!/ . . . Torches, torches! . . ." (Act II, Sc. 1, 33-34): those who want light least can call for it most loudly. Then Gloucester enters — how? ". . . with torches" (line 38) — the agent of light, but a kind of light — a physical reality like his eyes — that does him no good; it is inner illumination that he needs. It is at the end of this scene, finally, that Regan and Cornwall come to Gloucester's castle. They come, then, at night, a fact which we might easily pay no attention to if Shakespeare did not twice remind us of it. Edmund tells Edgar that Cornwall is coming, "now, i' th' night" (line 26); and then Regan's words add emphasis, "out of season, threading dark-ey'd night" — a phrase full of suggestion of things not seen and things not meant to be seen. Regan's thus coming into the sight pattern nicely amplifies the moral context: Regan joins Edmund among those who utilize the dark. These must always have a Gloucester — the not-seeing, or, better, the late-seeing.

For gradually Gloucester comes to see — in practical terms, too late. The first glimmerings come to him in Act III, Scene 3, when he tells Edmund of his decision to aid Lear. But even now, as we have seen, his motives are not altogether clear, and he is still in the dark about Edmund. In giving practical form to the allegiance to Lear upon which he has resolved, Gloucester again acts in the darkness of the night. In Act III, Scene 4 he hunts up Lear in the stormy night, just as he hunted for Edgar at night in Act II, Scene 1. This time he finds what he is looking for, and at the same time, so to speak, finds himself. The scene of his arrival on the heath is full of imaginative connections with other scenes. Just before Gloucester enters, the Fool says: "Now a little fire in a wild field were like an old lecher's heart — a small spark, all the rest on's body cold. Look, here comes a walking fire" (Act III, Sc. 4, 115-19). Since the play has opened with an account of Gloucester's lechery, it seems more than an accident that the Fool is given this particular simile just at the moment of Gloucester's entrance; we can hardly avoid reading it as a direct announcement of Gloucester. In another sense, too, the Fool's language is appropriate: Gloucester's heart has up until now been indeed but a "small spark," and, on the field of Lear's desolate situation, Gloucester's help is hardly more than "a little fire." Just at the moment when the Fool announces "a walking fire," Gloucester enters, significantly, "with a torch" (Act III, Sc. 4, 120). It is the only other time the play mentions lights. This time we feel that the torch is not ironic but symbolizes the first dim state of enlightenment: Gloucester is no longer blindly confident as he travels the way of the world, and he exhibits a growing sympathy with Lear and a moderation of his attitude to Edgar, whom he once called villain repeatedly (Act II, Sc. 1, 79 ff.) but of whom he now speaks in regret rather than anger (Act III, Sc. 4, 171ff.). As I have said, he finds himself. In Act III, Scene 6 he warns Lear of the plot against his life. Just when Gloucester is at last taking a stand which can have very serious consequences, whether or not he can foresee them entirely, Edmund's plot against him matures. The very first threat against him is Goneril's "Pluck out his eyes" (Act III, Sc. 7, 5) — the eyes which have given Gloucester so limited a perception as to make him partially adjust himself to Goneril's own regime. He is arrested; then follows the "trial" scene; and his eyes are put out. He is deprived of the organs which he once used so superficially. Yet this happens just as he is at last coming to real insight.

The fifty lines of dialogue which accompany the gouging out of Gloucester's eyes are full of verbal commentary upon what is happening and its meaning. Cornwall is brutally direct: "Upon these eyes of thine I'll set my foot" (Act III, Sc. 7, 68). There is a minor tension between the horrifyingly fierce wit of Regan, "One side will mock another. Th' other too!" (line 71) and the dying sally of the Servant who has attacked Cornwall and has been stabbed from the rear by Regan, "My lord, you have one eye left/To see some mischief on him" (lines 81-82) — which is at once a reminder of Gloucester's torture and yet the proffering of such comfort as may come from a slender hope of requital for the torturer. Repeatedly Cornwall betrays a mad passion to cut off the seeing process (lines 68, 72), especially at the moment when, fatally wounded, he puts out Gloucester's second eye. "Lest it see more, prevent it" (line 83). Each remark of his picks up a *see* from the preceding speaker: he is frenzied by the thought, which hardly takes clear form in his mind, of what Gloucester has seen.

Cornwall's ferocity here is in excellent contrast with his bathetically considerate dismissal, a little earlier, of Edmund, who is almost equally callous. Even this dismissal is done in terms of the sight imagery. It is just after Goneril has called "Pluck out his eyes" that Cornwall speaks thus to Edmund. "The revenges we are bound to take upon your traitorous father are not fit for your beholding" (lines 7-9). Such considerateness sets off, also, the real, costly compassion which Gloucester has for Lear: and this is the heart of the scene — the growing insight of Gloucester. Gloucester is defensive at first, perhaps a little uncertain; but at last he recognizes the moment of decision. Questioned, he answers Regan, "Because I would not see thy cruel nails/ Pluck out his poor old eyes; . . . " (lines 56-57), his words ironically anticipating his own fate. He even becomes consciously prophetic, "But I shall see/The winged vengeance overtake such children" (lines 65-66). The former peacemaker, once a little in awe of Gloucester, has thrown off his old character. Then Gloucester, "dark and comfortless" (lines 85) as in the earlier night scenes, begs Edmund — who is physically absent now as he was spiritually deficient before, and whose physical absence Gloucester cannot see just as before he could not detect his spiritual shortcoming — to "enkindle all the sparks of nature" (line 86) to avenge him: Edmund is to be both a fire and a light. Instead, Gloucester ironically receives from Regan his climactic enlightenment: it was Edmund who " made the overture" (line 89) of Gloucester's treason, that is, laid it open to the eyes of Goneril and Regan. Yet the real climax comes in Gloucester's answer. Gloucester does not dwell on Edmund's treachery; in fact, he does not refer to Edmund at this moment or ever again. From now on, he is concerned about his own dreadful mistake and the wrong he has done Edgar. His words are,

> O my follies! Then Edgar was abused.
> Kind gods, forgive me that, and prosper him!
>
> (lines 91-92)

Gloucester has leapt immediately to the truth about Edgar, as he might have done when Edmund first made his accusation. Then, he avoided the hard work of consulting Edgar's life — the true image of his character. Now, in his act of inference we see that his imagination — long dulled, or perhaps never active — is at work: insight comes to him. He whom Cornwall calls an "eyeless villain" (line 96) sees at last.

The blinding of Gloucester is at once an act of vengeance by the tyrants, an expiatory suffering by Gloucester, and an ironic commentary upon human experience. In his final character it transcends the concocted irony which at first glance the coincidence of Gloucester's coming to insight and his being blinded might be mistaken for. The irony is not a put-up effect but is inseparable from a profound writer's attitude to his materials. "Out, vile jelly!/Where is thy lustre now?" (lines 83-84) — Cornwall's words of triumph imply, as the speeches of Shakespeare's villains often do, more than he suspects. What Cornwall does not know is that Gloucester now sees better than he has ever seen; perhaps the final guarantee of his insight is his loss of outward sight. The vile jelly, the material seeing, had but caught reflections from the outer surfaces of life; as long as these were available to him, the seeing Gloucester was spiritually blind. The sisters and Cornwall cut him off from this outer world, which, as we know, circumscribed his vision; hence their fury is self-defeating, for they give him what their general conduct has already prepared him for — inward vision. His physical and material loss is spiritual gain: he who would find his life must lose it.

This is a basic paradox of the play. It is one of a series of paradoxes which, developed by the patterns, are the main structural determinants of *King Lear*. To have eyes, and to see not, is to be at the mercy of evil, and thus to aid evil. Not to see is not to understand: the sight pattern prepares us for the study of evil that finds its main treatment in the madness pattern. . . .

The Sight Pattern: Lear

Gloucester, we have seen, is imposed upon, whereas Lear imposes; and this relationship we should keep clear. But what one imposes on other people is also a reflection of one's insight — insight into the implications of what one does, and into those upon whom one imposes something. Lear's problem, then, we might also expect to be underlined by the sight pattern, and it is; and the applicability of the same poetic terms to both protagonists is one evidence of thematic kinship between them and thus of the unity of the play.

Lear, of course, is treated primarily in terms of the understanding, and the paradox of his wisdom is that it is concomitant with madness — a stroke of genius that raises the whole problem of the uses and limits of rationalism. But the madness pattern is enriched by the support of the sight pattern, which exhibits Lear as progressing, not from a blind sight to a seeing blindness, like Gloucester, but from an unwillingness to see, through a period of gradual anguished enlightenment, to a final passionate struggle to see. Early in the play Lear, blinded by anger, orders Kent, "Out of my sight!" (Act I, Sc. 1, 159); there is more than chance in these words, for Kent picks them up immediately with, "See better, Lear, and let me still remain/The true blank of thine eye" (lines 160-61). Kent sees what is involved; Lear does not. His vision called in question, Lear swears, ironically, by Apollo — the god of light; and Kent retorts, ". . . by Apollo, . . ./Thou swear'st thy gods in vain" (lines 162-63); both invoke the power of light, and Kent obeys only on an oath by Jupiter, the overriding absolute (line 181). Now, in another example of Shakespeare's regular use of parallelism of scenes, this episode is replayed, as it were, with variations, late in the play, where the effect combines irony and pathos: at the end of the play, Lear can hardly recognize Kent physically, as before he could not "see" Kent's moral quality and ordered him out of his sight. "Mine eyes are not o' th' best," he says, and "This' a dull sight" and "I'll see that straight" (Act V, Sc. 3, 279, 282, 287). Kent cannot comfort and aid Lear now just as, though he was willing enough, he could not give him needed help at the beginning. Suitably Kent comments, "All's cheerless, dark, and deadly" (line 290). The meaning of Lear's words extends far beyond the immediate context; they call into play again the paradox of experience embodied in Gloucester's history: he who is sure of his sight needs to question it, but he with a sense of "dull sight" in the world may see sharply within.

For if Lear is not clear about physical identities, he is now fairly straight about moral identities: he comes both to recognize Cordelia and to know what she stands for. The treatment of the Lear-Cordelia relationship forges a still more powerful sight link between first and final scenes. In Act I Lear says,

. . . for we

> Have no such daughter, nor shall ever see
> That face of hers again.   (Act I, Sc. 1, 265-67)

He is, as we have said, banishing a part of himself, determining to be blind. But, as Lear is bitterly enlightened, the face becomes a symbol of the sole value worth having, and Lear not only comes to want to see that face again but at the end passionately studies it, searching for a sign of life. "Lend me a looking-glass," he cries (Act V, Sc. 3, 261); it is to be for him a mirror of physical life, and a mirror of the life of the spirit. His words also recall the joke of the Fool, "For there was never yet fair woman but she made mouths in a glass" (Act III, Sc. 2, 35-36). But this fair woman, far from looking at herself, can make no kind of sign for others to see. Just before he dies, Lear strains frantically, possibly convinced that he does see life:

> Do you see this? Look on her, look, her lips,
> Look there, look there!   (Act V, Sc. 3, 310-11)

The frenzied searching of the face which he had once said he would never see again is a symbol of how his seeing, and the impulses that direct his seeing, have improved. Once he tossed light away; now, in the darkness of Act V, he seeks — and perhaps finds, for a moment — the illuminating love which came to Gloucester in his blindness. "Look up," Edgar says (Act V, Sc. 3, 312), but the time for looking has given way to sightless death.

Between these opening and closing scenes there is, in Lear's experience, an unremitting stress upon darkness, a stress which permits us to feel still further the effects of the sight pattern. Always we are reminded of the tragic failure to see the truth in time — the failure of those who had the power of sight but did not use it. "So out went the candle, and we were left darkling," says the Fool in apparent jest (Act I, Sc. 4, 237); yet *darkling* is rich in overtones. It is at this time in the play that — with Shakespeare's usual irony — Lear is beginning to regain his lost vision. In a few seconds he asks, of himself,

>   Where are his eyes?
> Either his notion weakens, his discernings
> Are lethargied . . .   (lines 247-49)

his words are almost the equivalent of Gloucester's "I stumbled when I saw." "Alack, the night comes on," Gloucester says (Act II, Sc. 4, 303) — the night which is the penalty for blindness, even though a little light is now coming through to the blind. Lear swears, "Darkness and devils" (Act I, Sc. 4, 273), and Edgar carries the hint a bit further with remarks on the "prince of darkness" (Act III, Sc. 4, 148; 6, 7-9). In a distraught world even casual phrases reflect the kind of ill it suffers from, for it is the darkness, the failure to see, that is diabolical. Lear asks where his eyes have been; then he swears, as it were, by the very blindness that is the source of the evil. These words are spoken in the storm and dark night — it is notable how much important action takes place in the dark night — and then Lear falls gradually into mental darkness. Yet this darkness, instead of being a merciful blotting out of evil sights, brings with it paradoxically a new intensity of imaginative illumination. Like Gloucester, Lear sees better when normal faculties are gone. A terrible darkness and a terrible light coincide. Shakespeare makes this point explicitly in terms of the sight imagery: he has the physician tell Cordelia that his medicine "Will close the eye of anguish" (Act IV, Sc. 4, 15). Sleeping will cut off a burning vision — yet help restore a normal sight which cannot discern much less than anguish. Still, after this protracted dark night, it is peculiarly right that almost the first words of Lear, after his restorative sleep, are, "Fair daylight?" (Act IV, Sc. 7, 52). At one level, of course, the words convey incredulity and sense of relief. But his inquiry opens a group of lines which symbolize the change in his power of seeing. He continues:

> I should e'en die with pity,
> To see another thus. I know not what to say.
> I will not swear these are my hands. Let's see, . . .
> COR.   Oh, look upon me, sir,
> And hold your hands in benediction o'er me.
>   (Act IV, Sc. 7, 53-55, 57-58)

He can see compassionately; he can inquire — "Let's see" instead of insisting upon his own correctness with proud obstinacy (we recall that Gloucester, when he said, "Let's see," was being gulled, and Edgar used the same words when he was skillfully managing a situation); and he can look upon Cordelia, whom once he wanted never to see again. Of what she stands for, he will not lose sight again; yet in seeing her he will have to go through a final agony.

Lear's Daughters

What must man see? How shall he see? Shakespeare constantly labored at the question, and in a sense he came early to a specific problem of modern civilization, which from his time to ours has been casting old insights overboard and looking for replacements. At times the problem phrases itself for Shakespeare as the problem of innocence, to which he devoted himself more that once. Innocence — not seeing enough — may itself be a gateway to evil. Othello and Desdemona are the primary innocents. Gloucester and Edgar act on a different plane, of course, yet a little more of the serpent in either would have been practically useful to both. But in Shakespeare there is an unfailing use of counterpoint: there is always the glance at the other extreme. If failure to see is dangerous, seeing too well may be fatal: the lost souls in *King Lear* are those who see too well. Goneril and Regan have freed themselves of the old insights and learned to look sharply at the immediate world; they see nothing of spirit, but they miss few of the close facts of experience. There may therefore be more content than we normally assume in the hyperbolic assurance made to Lear by the sharp-eyed Goneril — she who later shrieks, as her sentence upon Gloucester, "Pluck out his eyes!" — that she loves him "dearer than eyesight". (Act I, Sc. 1, 57) — the words which actually introduce the sight pattern in the play. What kind of eyesight that is exactly defined by a subsequent phrase applied by Cordelia to her sisters, "still-soliciting eye" (Act I, Sc. 1, 234), and by Goneril's own words to Regan, "You see how full of changes his age is. The observation we have made of it hath not been little" (lines 291-92). That is, they see what the situation is and know how to manage it; indeed, they see things only too clearly. But the deficiencies of their shrewd kind of observation are not left merely to inference: Shakespeare points directly at them in Albany's "How far your eyes may pierce I cannot tell" (Act I, Sc. 4, 368) and in the Fool's ditty, "Fathers that wear rags/Do make their children blind" (Act II, Sc. 4, 48-49). Even these casual lines call our attention to a myopia that has spread ironically through a society. Yet the sisters' deficiency of sight is a very special case, for it is they who especially practice a realistic looking at things; here is one first suggestion of a counterpoint to the paradox of the blinded Gloucester who has insight — namely, the paradox of blindness in those who see too well.

To say that one's way of seeing things is an index of character is a truism; yet the truism lights up with poetic energy when it becomes identified with the patterns in *King Lear*. When he comes to understand her (she "Look'd black upon me," he says — Act II, Sc. 4, 162), Lear curses Goneril thus: "You nimble lightnings, dart your blinding flames/Into her scornful eyes!" (lines 167-68). This packed speech not only places Goneril more clearly in the system of meanings of the play (her "scornful eyes" symbolize her view of the moral values assumed by Lear and the others), but also sets up a double irony: it is not she who is blinded (she is already *blind*), but Gloucester who is blinded by her, and not she, but Lear himself, who is exposed to the lightning. The irony takes a new tack a few lines later when Lear, speaking to Regan of Goneril, compares the sisters: "Her eyes are fierce; but thine/Do comfort and not burn" (lines 175-76). But these fierce eyes, which Lear will soon find that Regan shares, do not look ahead: they do not sense retribution. In the imaginary trial scene in the farmhouse, Edgar says, "Look, where he stands and glares! Want'st thou eyes at trial, madam?" (Act III, Sc. 6, 25-26) that is, can you not see the foul fiend? A minute later Lear reinvokes the original symbol for his inevitable recantation of trust in Regan's kindness: her "warp'd looks proclaim/What store her heart is made on" (lines 56-57).

What comes of scornful and fierce eyes and warped looks? The distortion of experience which they bring to the minds behind them must ultimately incapacitate those minds. It is beautifully ironic that just when Albany has emerged from what we may assume to be a difficult conflict of loyalties and has come to see Goneril as she is, Goneril should sneer at him as a man "Who hast not in thy brows an eye discerning/Thine honour from thy suffering" (Act IV, Sc. 2, 52-53). We recognize the human pattern:

Goneril wants Albany to be blind, for it is to her convenience that he does not see many things: yet the reassuring conviction that he is blind — which takes the paradoxical form of an accusation — serves for the first time to dull her practical sight: she does not detect in him a moral ally of the opposing forces. Or to put it another way: the great difficulty of true perception appears in the clear-sighted evil person's inability to recognize goodness in another; from such a failure may come insuperable danger. In fact, Goneril and her sister have got caught in a complex of self-betrayals, chief of which is their passion for Edmund: at the end all they can see is each other. The sight pattern demonstrates that this new turn is a logical continuation of the path they have already traveled. Regan suspects Goneril: "She gave strange eliads and most speaking looks/To noble Edmund" (Act IV, Sc. 5, 25-26): the hard realistic eye engages in love play. When Regan intimates that she may marry Edmund, Goneril retorts, "That eye that told you so look'd but asquint' (Act V, Sc. 3, 72). Without knowing it Goneril, who often phrases keen truths, actually summarizes, in this speech which comes close to the end, what the play has been saying about Regan and herself. One kind of eyesight was very dear to them; yet those who trust only to the outer eye and deny the inner find themselves, at the end, looking asquint.

Shakespeare has found in sight a flexibly responding symbol for the problems which arise in connection with the point of view from which man judges the meaning of experience. He enriches his commentary on the problems by another use of his symbolic pattern, which heightens the contrast between the sisters and Cordelia. They look hard, scornful, fierce. But as early as Act I Cordelia can say she leaves "with wash'd eyes". (Act I, Sc.1, 271) — in tears, perhaps, but also cleansed of any mote that might deflect her clear view of her sisters. Later her eyes are wet with tears; the tears which denote sympathy are themselves a way of looking at experience. Gloucester condemns the man who "will not see/Because he does not feel"; shortly after his speech, Cordelia exemplifies the human being who sees because she does feel (Act IV, Sc.3, 20). She feels compassion and cries; the tears come from the eyes; feeling and seeing are identified. Lear urges her not to cry (Act IV, Sc. 7, 71; Act V, Sc. 3, 23); and he constantly fights his own tears (Act II, Sc. 4, 28 off.; Act IV, Sc. 6, 199-201). For a king, tears would be a surrender, a way of seeing failure, giving comfort to the point of view of those in control. With dry eyes he will observe what he missed before. And in resisting one impulse to cry he makes a self-criticism that has a double value: he threatens to "pluck out," if they weep again, his "old fond eyes" (Act I, Sc. 4, 323-24). As it turns out, it is not his eyes that are plucked out, but Gloucester's — because he did not finally surrender, but did show compassion to a public enemy. But the eyes which are "fond" because they would weep have already been "fond" in another way: we are reminded again of Lear's original blindness.

Chorus

By a full and varied use of all the functions of men's eyes Shakespeare has achieved a rich, multivalued symbolic expression of man's moral make-up. Kent, whose detachment and courage are set forth in the sight imagery, uses a proverbial saying for a comment on Lear's ironic fate.

> Good King, that must approve the common saw,
> Thou out of Heaven's benediction comest
> To the warm sun!   (Act II, Sc. 2, 167-69)

The king's experience, that is, burns him; but the sun is light, also, and Lear, by suffering, receives illumination. Lear at first not only sees Cordelia in the wrong light, but encourages Burgundy to do likewise; the terms in which Cordelia and France comment upon Burgundy's view of Cordelia indicate that he is looking at her from the wrong point of view: his "regards" are "Aloof from th' entire point" (Act I, Sc. 1, 243). That is, his seeing is directed by the wrong values — . . . This line, then, and that of Kent's have a choral value; and the aptness of the symbol appears in its ability to be used chorally.

An effective chorus is never a flat statement which comes up with a two-plus-two-equals-four about the figures on the stage. It needs to be integral with the design, and wholly unselfconscious, and for that reason it comes best as a speech which belongs primarily to its own dramatic context but which, by its identification with the pattern of which the reader has become aware, transcends the context and becomes an imaginative commentary upon the whole world of the drama. When the Gentleman speaks of "impetuous blasts, with eyeless rage" (Act III, Sc. 1, 8), surely his words "eyeless rage" suggest the essence of various actions — primarily the unseeing passion of Lear, but also that of Gloucester, and that of Cornwall to come, and of the sisters still later: rages which are retribution and which call forth further retribution. When Edgar tells Gloucester that he can no longer look down the supposed cliff lest "the deficient sight/Topple down headlong" (Act IV, Sc. 6, 23-24), we can only think of the "deficient sight" that causes disaster throughout the play, and of those whom it has indeed toppled down headlong. When the Fool wittily exclaims, "All that follow their noses are led by their eyes but blind men . . ." (Act II, Sc. 4, 69-70), the very fact that he makes his statement as a general truth strengthens the reminder that in the world of the play there are few that follow their eyes, or that have eyes to follow. Lear and Gloucester are blind to the meaning of those phenomena which betoken the presence of evil; Edmund, Goneril, and Regan to the existence of moral barriers to the consummation of their ambitions. But the blind man cannot be tricked by his eyes; whereas those who pride themselves on clear sight may be misled both by the world they seem to control and by the appearance of well-being within themselves. And after so much rage, so many reversals, so much agony, so much searching for truth, it is fitting for Edgar to close by saying, "We that are young/Shall never see so much . . ."

An epoch has passed; the next stage in the cycle will be quieter and less searching.

What the sight pattern never lets us forget is the importance of man's way of looking at the world: the problem is not, "How shall the world be saved?" but "How shall the world be seen?"...

Selected Criticisms

So to see Lear acted, — to see an old man tottering about the stage with a walking-stick, turned out of doors by his daughters in a rainy night, has nothing in it but what is painful and disgusting. We want to take him into shelter and relieve him. That is all the feeling which the action of *Lear* ever produced in me. But the *Lear* of Shakespeare cannot be acted. The contemptible machinery by which they mimic the storm which he goes out in, is not more inadequate to represent the horrors of the real elements, than any actor can be to represent Lear; they might more easily propose to personate the Satan of Milton upon a stage, or one of Michael Angelo's terrible figures. The greatness of Lear is not in corporal dimension, but in intellectual: the explosions of passion are terrible as a volcano: they are storms turning up and disclosing to the bottom that sea his mind, with all its vast riches. It is his mind which is laid bare. This case of flesh and blood seems too insignificant to be thought on; even as he himself neglects it. On the stage we see nothing but corporal infirmities and weakness, the impotence of rage; while we read it, we see not Lear, but we are Lear, — we are in his mind, we are sustained by a grandeur which baffles the malice of daughters and storms; in the aberrations of his reason, we discover a mighty irregular power of reasoning, immethodized from the ordinary purposes of life, but exerting its powers, as the wind blows where it listeth, at will upon the corruptions and abuses of mankind.

Charles Lamb

The modern practice of blending comedy with tragedy, though liable to great abuse in point of practice, is undoubtedly an extension of the dramatic circle; but the comedy should be as in *King Lear*, universal, ideal, and sublime. It is perhaps the intervention of this principle which determines the balance in favour of *King Lear* against *Oedipus Tyrannus* or the *Agamemnon*, or, if you will, the trilogies with which they are connected; unless the intense power of the choral poetry, especially that of the latter, should be considered as restoring the equilibrium. *King Lear*, if it can sustain this comparison, may be judged to be the most perfect specimen of the dramatic art existing in the world; in spite of the narrow conditions to which the poet was subjected by the ignorance of the philosophy of the drama which has prevailed in modern Europe.

Percy Bysshe Shelley

King Lear deals especially with the natural man as opposed to the artificial man. When the King saw Edgar, then a Tom o' Bedlam, in the great storm scene, he exclaims — "Is man no more than this? Consider him well. Thou owest the worm no silk, the beast no hide, the sheep no wool, the cat no perfume. Ha! here's three on's (himself, the Fool, Kent) are sophisticated! Thou art the thing itself: unaccomodated man is no more but such a poor, bare, forked animal as thou art. Off, off, you lendings! Come; unbutton here." And he tears his clothes off him. And this bare-stripped figure, in that awful scene, may serve as an image of the society the play represents. It is a society with all its disguises torn off. The passions walk abroad, bold and confident. Greed lifts up its head unabashed; Lust scorns all holy ties; Wrath rages like a tempest. A fearful earth, indeed, if given over to such accursed powers! But it is not so. There is also the passion of Love, and throughout the play love is performing its secret ministry. Good and evil close in a fierce struggle, as always where there is life, and not mere death; and in the end good prevails, as in the end it must prevail: for evil has not only good to encounter, but it has to fight with itself: it is essentially self-consuming. So that in this play we have presented to us humanity in its purest and simplest elements — humanity unsophisticated, denuded of all its "lendings," with its natural impulses all unchecked and potent.

John W. Hales

The Tragedy of Lear is deservedly celebrated among the dramas of Shakespeare. There is perhaps no play which keeps the attention so strongly fixed; which so much agitates our passions and interests our curiosity. The artful involutions of distinct interests, the striking opposition of contrary characters, the sudden changes of fortune, and the quick succession of events, fill the mind with a perpetual tumult of indignation, pity, and hope. There is no scene which does not contribute to the aggravation of the distress or conduct of the action, and scarce a line which does not conduce to the progress of the scene. So powerful is the current of the poet's imagination, that the mind, which once ventures within it, is hurried irresistibly along.

On the seeming improbability of Lear's conduct it may be observed, that he is represented according to histories at that time vulgarly received as true. And perhaps if we turn our thoughts upon the barbarity and ignorance of the age to which this story is referred, it will appear not so unlikely as while we estimate Lear's manners by our own. Such preference of one daughter to another, or resignation of dominion on such conditions, would be yet credible, if told of a petty prince of Guinea or Madagascar. Shakespeare, indeed, by the mention of his Earls and Dukes, has given us the idea of times more civilised, and of life regulated by softer manners; and the truth is, that though he so nicely discriminates, and so minutely describes the characters of men, he commonly neglects and confounds the characters of ages, by mingling customs ancient and modern, English and foreign.

My learned friend Mr. Warton, who has in the *Adventurer* very minutely criticised this play, remarks, that the instances of cruelty are too savage and shocking, and that the intervention of Edmund destroys the simplicity of the story. These objections may, I think, be answered, by repeating, that the cruelty of the daughters is an historical fact, to which the poet has added little, having only drawn it into a series by dialogue and action. But I am not able to apologise with equal plausibility for the extrusion of Gloucester's eyes, which seems an act too horrid to be endured in dramatick exhibition, and such as must always compel the mind to relieve its distress by incredulity. Yet let it be remembered that our authour well knew what would please the audience for which he wrote.

The injury done by Edmund to the simplicity of the action is abundantly recompensed by the addition of variety, by the art with which he is made to co-operate with the chief design, and the opportunity which he gives the poet of combining perfidy with perfidy, and connecting the wicked son with the wicked daughters, to impress this important moral, that villainy is never at a stop, that crimes lead to crimes, and at last terminate in ruin.

But though this moral be incidentally enforced, Shakespeare has suffered the virtue of Cordelia to perish in a just cause, contrary to the natural ideas of justice, to the hope of the reader, and, what is yet more strange, to the faith of chronicles. Yet this conduct is justified by the Spectator, who blames Tate for giving Cordelia success and happiness in his alteration, and declares, that, in his opinion, the tragedy has lost half its beauty. . . . A play in which the wicked prosper, and the virtuous miscarry, may doubtless be good, because it is a just representation of the common events of human life: but since all reasonable beings naturally love justice, I cannot easily be persuaded, that the observation of justice makes a play worse; or, that if other excellencies are equal, the audience will not always rise better pleased from the final triumph of persecuted virtue.

In the present case the publick has decided. Cordelia, from the time of Tate, has always retired with victory and felicity. And, if my sensations could add any thing to the general suffrage, I might relate, that I was many years ago so shocked by Cordelia's death, that I know not whether I ever endured to read again the last scenes of the play till I undertook to revise them as an editor.

There is another controversy among the criticks concerning this play. It is disputed whether the predominant image in Lear's disordered mind be the loss of his kingdom or the cruelty of his daughters. Mr. Murphy, a very judicious critic has evinced by induction of particular passages, that the cruelty of his daughters is the primary source of his distress, and that the loss of royalty affects him only as a secondary and subordinate evil; he observes with great justness, that Lear would move our compassion but little, did we not rather consider the injured father than the degraded king. . . .

Samuel Johnson

We wish that we could pass this play over, and say nothing about it. All that we can say must fall far short of the subject; or even of what we ourselves conceive of it. To attempt to give a description of the play itself or of its effect upon the mind, is mere impertinence: yet we must say something. — It is then the best of all Shakespear's plays, for it is the one in which he was the most in earnest. He was here fairly caught in the web of his own imagination. The passion which he has taken as his subject is that which strikes its root deepest into the human heart; of which the bond is the hardest to be unloosed; and the cancelling and tearing to pieces of which gives the greatest revulsion to the frame. This depth of nature, this force of passion, this tug and war of the elements of our being, this firm faith in filial piety, and the giddy anarchy and whirling tumult of the thoughts at finding this prop failing it, the contrast between the fixed, immoveable basis of natural affection, and the rapid, irregular starts of imagination, suddenly wrenched from all its accustomed holds and resting-places in the soul, this is what Shakespear has given, and what nobody else but he could give. So we believe. — The mind of Lear, staggering between the weight of attachment and the hurried movements of passion, is like a tall ship driven about by the winds, buffeted by the furious waves, but that still rides above the storm, having its anchor fixed in the bottom of the sea; or it is like the sharp rock circled by the eddying whirlpool that foams and beats against it, or like the solid promontory pushed from its basis by the force of an earthquake.

The character of Lear itself is very finely conceived for the purpose. It is the only ground on which such a story could be built with the greatest truth and effect. It is his rash-haste, his violent impetuosity, his blindness to everything but the dictates of his passions or affections, that produces all his misfortunes, that aggravates his impatience of them, that enforces our pity for him. The part which Cordelia bears in the scene is extremely beautiful: the story is almost told in the first words she utters. We see at once the precipice on which the poor old king stands from his own extravagant and credulous importunity, the indiscreet simplicity of her love (which, to be sure, has a little of her father's obstinacy in it) and the hollowness of her sisters' pretensions. Almost the first burst of that noble tide of passion, which runs through the play, is in the remonstrance of Kent to his royal master on the injustice of his sentence against his youngest daughter — "Be Kent unmannerly, when Lear is mad!" This manly plainness, which draws down on him the displeasure of the unadvised king, is worthy of the fidelity with which he adheres to his fallen fortunes. The true character of the two eldest daughters, Regan and Gonerill (they are so thoroughly hateful that we do not even like to repeat their names) breaks out in their answer to Cordelia who desires them to treat their father well — "Prescribe not us our duties" — their hatred of advice being in proportion to their determination to do wrong, and to their hypocritical pretensions to do right. Their deliberate hypocrisy adds the last finishing to the odiousness of their characters. It is the absence of this detestable quality that is the only relief in the character of Edmund the Bastard, and that at times reconciles us to him. We are not tempted to exaggerate the guilt of his conduct, when he himself gives it up as a bad business, and writes himself down "plain villain." Nothing more can be said about it. His religious honesty in this respect is admirable. . . . The whole character, its careless, light-hearted villainy, contrasted with the sullen, rancorous malignity of Regan and Gonerill, its connection with the conduct of the under-plot, in which Gloster's persecution of one of his sons and the ingratitude of another, form a counterpart to the mistakes and misfortunes of Lear, — his double amour with the two sisters, and the share which he has in bringing about the fatal catastrophe, are all managed with an uncommon degree of skill and power.

It has been said, and we think justly, that the third act of *Othello* and the three first acts of *Lear*, are Shakespear's great master-pieces in the logic of passion: that they contain the highest examples not only of the force of individual passion, but of its dramatic vicissitudes and striking effects arising from the different circumstances and characters of the persons speaking. We see the ebb and flow of the feeling, its pauses and feverish starts, its impatience of opposition, its accumulating force when it has time to recollect itself, the manner in which it avails itself of every passing word or gesture, its haste to repel insinuation, the alternate contraction and dilatation of the soul, and all "the dazzling fence of controversy" in this mortal combat with poisoned weapons, aimed at the heart, where each wound is fatal. We have seen in *Othello*, how the unsuspecting frankness and impetuous passions of the Moor are played upon and exasperated by the artful dexterity of Iago. In the present play, that which aggravates the sense of sympathy in the reader, and of uncontrollable anguish in the swollen heart of Lear, is the petrifying indifference, the cold, calculating, obdurate selfishness of his daughters. His keen passions seem whetted on their stony hearts. The contrast would be too painful, the shock too great, but for the intervention of the Fool, whose well-timed levity comes in to break the continuity of feeling when it can no longer be borne, and to bring into play again the fibres of the heart just as they are growing rigid from over-strained excitement. The imagination is glad to take refuge in the half-comic, half-serious comments of the Fool, just as the mind under the extreme anguish of a surgical operation vents itself in sallies of wit. The character was also a grotesque ornament of the barbarous times, in which alone the tragic ground-work of the story could be laid. In another point of view it is indispensable, inasmuch as while it is a diversion to the too great intensity of our disgust, it carries the pathos to the highest pitch of which it is capable, by shewing the pitiable weakness of the old king's conduct and its irretrievable consequences in the most familiar point of view. Lear may well "beat at the gate which let his folly in," after, as the Fool says, "he has made his daughters his mothers." The character is dropped in the third act to make room for the entrance of Edgar as Mad Tom, which well accords with the increasing bustle and wildness of the incidents; and nothing can be more complete than the distinction between Lear's real and Edgar's assumed madness, while the resemblance in the cause of their distresses, from the severing of the nearest ties of natural affection, keeps up a unity of interest. Shakespear's mastery over his subject, if it was not art, was owing to a knowledge of the connecting links of the passions, and their effect upon the mind, still more wonderful than any systematic adherence to rules, and that anticipated and outdid all the efforts of the most refined art, not inspired and rendered instinctive by genius.

One of the most perfect displays of dramatic power is the first interview between Lear and his daughter, after the designed affronts upon him, which till one of his knights reminds him of them, his sanguine temperament had led him to overlook. . . .

This is certainly fine: no wonder that Lear says after it, "O let me not be mad, not mad, sweet heavens," feeling its effects by anticipation; but fine as is this burst of rage and indignation at the first blow aimed at his hopes and expectations, it is nothing near so fine as what follows from his double disappointment, and his lingering efforts to see which of them he shall lean upon for support and find comfort in, when both his daughters turn against his age and weakness. It is with some difficulty that Lear gets to speak with his daughter Regan, and her husband, at Gloster's castle. In concert with Gonerill they have left their own home on purpose to avoid him. His apprehensions are first alarmed by this circumstance, and when Gloster, whose guests they are, urges the fiery temper of the Duke of Cornwall as an excuse for not importuning him a second time, Lear breaks out —

> Vengeance! Plague! Death! Confusion! —
> Fiery? What quality? Why, Gloster, Gloster,
> I'd speak with the Duke of Cornwall, and his wife.

Afterwards, feeling perhaps not well himself, he is inclined to admit their excuse from illness, but then recollecting that they have set his messenger (Kent) in the stocks, all his suspicions are roused again, and he insists on seeing them. . . .

[Hazlitt now quotes Act II, Scene 4, lines 129-289, ending with the following speech:]

> **Lear.** O, reason not the need: our basest beggars
> Are in the poorest thing superfluous:
> Allow not nature more than nature needs,
> Man's life is cheap as beast's: thou art a lady;
> If only to go warm were gorgeous,
> Why, nature needs not what thou gorgeous wear'st;
> Which scarcely keeps thee warm. — But, for true need —
> You heavens, give me that patience which I need!

You see me here, you gods; a poor old man,
As full of grief as age; wretched in both!
If it be you that stir these daughters' hearts
Against their father, fool me not so much
To bear it tamely; touch me with noble anger!
O, let no woman's weapons, water-drops,
Stain my man's cheeks! — No, you unnatural hags,
I will have such revenges on you both,
That all the world shall — I will do such things —
What they are, yet I know not; but they shall be
The terrors of the earth. You think, I'll weep:
No, I'll not weep: —
I have full cause of weeping; but this heart
Shall break into a hundred thousand flaws,
Or e'er I'll weep: — O, fool, I shall go mad! —
[Exeunt Lear, Gloster, Kent, and Fool.]

If there is any thing in any author like this yearning of the heart, these throes of tenderness, this profound expression of all that can be thought and felt in the most heart-rendering situations, we are glad of it; but it is in some author that we have not read.

The scene in the storm, where he is exposed to all the fury of the elements, though grand and terrible, is not so fine, but the moralising scenes with Mad Tom, Kent and Gloster, are upon a par with the former. His exclamation in the supposed trial-scene of his daughters, "See the little dogs and all, Tray, Blanch, and Sweetheart, see they bark at me," his issuing his orders, "Let them anatomize Regan, see what breeds about her heart," and his reflection when he sees the misery of Edgar, "Nothing but his unkind daughters could have brought him to this," are in a style of pathos, where the extremest resources of the imagination are called in to lay open the deepest movements of the heart, which was peculiar to Shakespear. In the same style and spirit is his interrupting the Fool who asks "whether a madman be a gentleman or a yeoman," by answering "A king, a king." —

The indirect part that Gloster takes in these scenes where his generosity leads him to relieve Lear and resent the cruelty of his daughters, at the very time that he is himself instigated to seek the life of his son, and suffering under the sting of his supposed ingratitude, is a striking accompaniment to the situation of Lear. Indeed, the manner in which the threads of the story are woven together is almost as wonderful in the way of art as the carrying on the tide of passion, still varying and unimpaired, is on the score of nature. Among the remarkable instances of this kind are Edgar's meeting with his old blind father; the deception he practises upon him when he pretends to lead him to the top of Dover-cliff — "Come on, sir, here's the place," to prevent his ending his life and miseries together;

his encounter with the perfidious Steward whom he kills, and his finding the letter from Goneril to his brother upon him which leads to the final catastrophe, and brings the wheel of Justice "full circle home" to the guilty parties. The bustle and rapid succession of events in the last scenes is surprising. But the meeting between Lear and Cordelia is by far the most affecting part of them. It has all the wildness of poetry, and all the heart-felt truth of nature. The previous account of her reception of the news of his unkind treatment, her involuntary reproaches to her sisters, "Shame, ladies, shame," Lear's backwardness to see his daughter, the picture of the desolate state to which he is reduced, "Alack, 'tis he; why he was met even now, as mad as the vex'd sea, singing aloud," only prepare the way for and heighten our expectation of what follows, and assuredly this expectation is not disappointed when through the tender care of Cordelia he revives and recollects her. . . .

Almost equal to this in awful beauty is their consolation of each other when, after the triumph of their enemies, they are led to prison.

> **Cordelia**. We are not the first,
> Who, with best meaning, have incurr'd the worst.
> For thee, oppressed king, am I cast down;
> Myself could else out-frown false fortune's frown. —
> Shall we not see these daughters, and these sisters?
> **Lear**. No, no, no, no! Come, let's away to prison:
> We two alone will sing like birds i' the cage:
> When thou dost ask me blessing, I'll kneel down,
> And ask of thee forgiveness: so we'll live,
> And pray, and sing, and tell old tales, and laugh
> At gilded butterflies, and hear poor rogues
> Talk of court news; and we'll talk with them too —
> Who loses, and who wins; who's in, who's out; —
> And take upon us the mystery of things,
> As if we were God's spies: and we'll wear out,
> In a wall'd prison, packs and sects of great ones,
> That ebb and flow by the moon.
> **Edmund**. Take them away.
> **Lear**. Upon such sacrifices, my Cordelia,
> The gods themselves throw incense.

The concluding events are sad, painfully sad; but their pathos is extreme. The oppression of the feelings is relieved by the very interest we take in the misfortunes of others, and by the reflections to which they give birth. Cordelia is hanged in prison by the orders of the bastard Edmund, which are known too late to be countermanded, and Lear dies broken-hearted, lamenting over her.

> **Lear**. And my poor fool is hang'd! No, no, no life:

Why should a dog, a horse, a rat, have life,
And thou no breath at all? O, thou wilt come no more,
Never, never, never, never, never! —
Pray you, undo this button: thank you, sir.

He dies, and indeed we feel the truth of what Kent says on the occasion —

Vex not his ghost: O, let him pass! he hates him,
That would upon the rack of this rough world
Stretch him out longer.

. . . . . .

Four things have struck us in reading *Lear*:
1. That poetry is an interesting study, for this reason, that it relates to whatever is most interesting in human life. Whoever therefore has a contempt for poetry, has a contempt for himself and humanity.
2. That the language of poetry is superior to the language of painting; because the strongest of our recollections relate to feelings, not to faces.
3. That the greatest strength of genius is shewn in describing the strongest passions: for the power of the imagination, in works of invention, must be in proportion to the force of the natural impressions, which are the subject of them.
4. That the circumstance which balances the pleasure against the pain in tragedy is, that in proportion to the greatness of the evil, is our sense and desire of the opposite good excited; and that our sympathy with actual suffering is lost in the strong impulse given to our natural affections, and carried away with the swelling tide of passion, that gushes from and relieves the heart.

William Hazlitt

Review Questions and Answers

Question 1.
Sketch the characters of Kent and Edgar.

Answer
Kent is the embodiment of loyal service and devotion. During Lear's reign he was a faithful servant —

"My life I never held, but as a pawn
To wage against thine enemies" —

and after his unjust banishment he returned with dog-like loyalty to serve and watch over his master in the hour of trouble and stress which he foresaw might come. He was blunt even to rudeness.

"Be Kent unmannerly

When Lear is mad."

He was bold to the point of being brash, as he says of himself "having more man than wit", and he suffered for his boldness and had a "shameful lodging" for his pains.

For Kent, Lear is always "every inch a king". He never sees the failings of character or of age in his master which are apparent to others, and what is more, his own devotion to the king is so absorbing that until he has seen it he cannot believe in his daughters' shameful treatment of him.

We love Kent for loving Cordelia and for taking her part, but we find that his love for Cordelia is only a part of his love for the king, which is the passion of his life. And we love him too for that one touch of human weakness which he shows at the end, when he comes in to the king, who is absorbed in weeping over Cordelia, and craves for a word of recognition; kneeling before him he cries —

"O, my good master !"

The recognition was scant enough, but Kent's love and loyalty see only the stricken king and his last needs, and when he has passed from "this tough world" Kent says —

"I have a journey . . . shortly to go,
  My master calls me, I must not say no."

Edgar's character develops and improves in the course of the play. At first we feel angry with him for being so easily fooled by Edmund, but afterwards in the later scenes he has gained resourcefulness and a determination of purpose which we must admire. One striking characteristic in Edgar is his buoyancy, due partly to his natural temperament, but still more to his strong religious feelings. He never despairs, because he never loses sympathy with others. Therefore he, the outcast Bedlamite, comes forth as the preserver of Gloucester, and the avenger of the crimes of Edmund.

There is something in Edgar we feel we can depend upon, and Albany recognized that, when he chose him as one to

"Rule in this realm, and the gored state sustain."

Question 2.
Trace the gradual growth of Lear's insanity.
Answer
There are a few passages in the play which show us something of Lear before the story begins, and it will help us to understand the development of Lear's passion into madness to examine these.

At the end of the first scene Goneril speaks of her father's treatment of Cordelia as a gross error of judgment, and says:

"The best and soundest of his time hath been but rash," and then points out that with *such dispositions as he bears* he will cause them offence unless he is deprived of authority.

The opening words of the play reveal the fact that the king is changeable, but this may only be an infirmity of age. He himself tells us with his own lips that he is imperious and will tolerate no opposition to his will. When addressing Kent, who interfered to prevent the banishment of Cordelia, he says:

> "Thou hast sought to make us break our vow
> *Which we durst never yet*, and with strain'd pride,
> To come between our sentence and our power,
> *Which nor our nature* nor our place *can bear*."

In the play itself we may trace four great outbursts of passion, "hysterica passio" as the king names it.

(1) The first is in the opening scene, when disappointment at Cordelia's failure to please him by an open avowal of her deep true love causes his wrath to blind his reason. For Lear, wanting something and having it are the same thing, and finding himself deprived where he most expected to be gratified, he does not stop to think why, but is hurried by his passion into a prompt and dreadful revenge. We must admit that Lear's great love for Cordelia was terribly wounded by her failure, but this feeling was blended with and soon overwhelmed by rage that his will was crossed, and his plans for his own future upset.

> "I thought to set my rest
> On her kind nursery,"

he says, and he is forced to make quite a different arrangement. The fact that it is Cordelia who crosses his will only adds bitterness to rage.

At first he controls his feelings in short phrases, but soon he, who has never learned self-restraint, is overcome by passion, and in a rush of ungoverned fury he banishes and disinherits his once dearest child. He goes on from one reasonless act to another, raising his arm to strike Kent, then taking up the power he has just laid down to sentence him to banishment. His passion seems here to give force to his character; he speaks so strongly —

> "Better thou

Hadst not been born than not to have pleased me better;" and is so resolute —

> "I have sworn; I am firm."
> "We
> Have no such daughter, nor shall ever see
> That face of hers again."

(2) When next Lear appears we see that the consequences of his act of

senseless rage are beginning to fall upon him. Goneril knows her father's weakness, and has made her plans to thwart and enrage him. She uses Oswald, who by his insolence rouses the king's anger, so that he strikes him, and calls him names. When Goneril herself comes in we witness the rise of the second great wave of passion in Lear, and at the same time we perceive a new effect. Lear's passion is now of no help in overcoming obstacles, but bounces back at himself, and makes him strike his own head, and cry —

"O, Lear, Lear, Lear,
  Beat at this gate that let thy folly in,
  And thy dear judgment out."

Under the influence of this passion he pours forth a torrent of curses upon Goneril, and the next moment is ashamed that she should see how deeply her conduct moves him.

(3) A third wave of hysterical passion bursts over him as he sets out on the journey to Regan. Here we note that he seems to have fears that these passionate convulsions may affect his mind; and under the influence of this fear he exclaims —

"O, let me not be mad, not mad, sweet heaven!
  Keep me in temper: I would not be mad."

(4) On the king's arrival at Gloucester's castle we witness another painful outburst, and in this scene, too, we see a fresh symptom. It is the sight of Kent in the stocks which this time excites his passion, and the king tries in vain to control it.

"O, how this mother swells up toward my heart!
  Hysterica passio, down, thou climbing sorrow,
  Thy element's below."
"O me, my heart, my rising heart! But down!"

Then, when he is so upset by his daughter's unkindness that he is unable to bear the strain, the first sign of failure shows itself in his beginning to harp on one idea, repeating at every pause his question —

"Who put my man i' the stocks?
          . . . . . .
Who stock'd my servant?
          . . . . . .
How came my man i' the stocks?"

After this, when we see him in the storm pouring forth his own stormy eloquence, full of matter, but with no coherency, we know that his reason is on the verge of complete breakdown. The breakdown actually occurs when the king comes in contact with the Bedlam beggar, from which time his hysterical passion becomes downright madness.

Question 3.

Identify and discuss the catastrophe in the central portion of *King Lear*.

Answer

In the scene in Gloucester's castle we see King Lear struggling with himself, trying to keep his mind either in calmness or under the influence of "noble anger"; but as unkindness follows unkindness, and insult follows insult, he is finally overwhelmed by his feelings, and can no longer contain himself. In majestic eloquence he calls on the heavens to give him patience, and then, as the idea suggests itself that the heavens themselves are in league with his two daughters, he appeals to them instead to endow him with noble anger. And for a moment it seems as if his passion comes once more to his aid as he threatens to have terrible revenge on these daughters. But his passion is now unable to sustain itself or him for long, and he turns to his one friend with the heart-rending cry —

"O, fool, I shall go mad,"

and rushes out into the night.

As the door opens we hear the awful storm which is raging , and when the king is again brought before us (Act III, Sc. 2 and 4) the explosions of his passion seem to merge themselves in the bursts of rain and thunder. In his desperation he calls on the elements to destroy him —

"You sulphurous and thought-executing fires,
. . . .
Singe my white head."

He seems to be raving, and yet there is a good deal of sense though no coherency in his utterances; he is not as yet quite mad; he raves in the desperate manner of one who is truly in sorrow. When Kent comes to him and advises him to take shelter in a hovel, he is in reality leading his master where he will meet with that which causes the final breakdown of his mental faculties. Until he comes into actual contact with a madman, the king is not really mad; but when on approaching the hovel where Edgar, in his assumed character of a Bedlam beggar, is concealed, he hears this lunatic's ravings, and sees his miserable plight, imitation sets in; he begins to talk in the same idiotic way, and even imitates Edgar in outward action too, beginning even in the cold rain to strip off his clothes. Thus we see him brought to a complete downfall. His powerfulness has gone, his majesty has gone, and now last of all his reason, and we see him in the most pitiful condition in which a man can be. The sightless Gloucester is rich in comparison, for he still possesses his reason; and so is Edgar, who seems to have nothing he can call has own, for even the loss of honour and trust is slight when viewed together with the heart-rending loss of the king. It is here that the victims of the two plots are brought together; the old king scarcely able to stand in the tempest, his white hairs caught by the windy blasts, and Edgar, to whose young strength the storm was not as overpowering, standing shivering before him in his madman's rags. We get two opposite effects from the working of the two plots into each other at this point, which may be said to mark the climax of the catastrophe. Through the wrongs and sufferings of Edgar we can get some slight comparative idea of the anguish of Lear; and at the same time it is a positive relief to the feelings to find that Lear has a friend. Again we notice how the poet has brought forward for the two chief sufferers, Lear and Gloucester, relief and help. For Lear help is to come from Cordelia through Kent; and for Gloucester a friend is found in his wronged son Edgar, who in his disguise hears those words of his father's which make known to him that he has been abused; so the disguise into which Edgar shifted for his own protection is now to become the means by which he is enabled to serve his father.

So in this central portion we have the climax of the catastrophe, and at the same time hopes of relief. We have, as it were, focussed into this portion the complete breaking down of all the bands of nature; every rule is broken, every tie is severed. The physical world is in convulsion, the moral world is convulsed by crime, and there is convulsion too in the world of reason.

Question 4.
Sketch the characters of Gloucester and Albany.

Answer
Gloucester and *Albany* are the two characters who stand between the purely good and utterly bad characters. Neither of them are particularly interesting, and about Gloucester there is a certain indefiniteness; it is difficult to point out his special characteristics, except superstitiousness and gullibility. In the course of the play his conscience is awakened, and he sees sin and its consequences in their true light. His is not a strong character like Kent's. He failed to support Kent in trying to dissuade the king from his folly with regard to the division of the kingdom, although he was at the time conscious that it was folly; but instead of opposing it he blamed the sun, the moon, and the stars; his superstitious beliefs prevent his acting in a manly way. But he was not without courage, and he shows himself strongly opposed to wrong when he denounces Cornwall and Regan for their cruelty to the king, and when, in spite of their threats, he works to relieve his master. So that as we watch him through the action of the play, we find him gradually strengthening in his adherence to the side of right, and he dies a wiser and a better man than he was at the beginning.

Albany seems, too, to come gradually to the side of right. That his conduct was not always good we know from the fact that the knight tells Lear that Albany, as well as Goneril, has shown an "abatement of kindness" towards him. But when once he has become undeceived about Goneril, and sees that her beauty is the outward mask of a ruthless fiend, he shows "honourable mettle", detaches himself from his wife's schemes, and in the end we see him trying to gather to himself those whom he knows to be worthy and noble. His justice and manliness after the battle are decidedly striking. While acknowledging Edmund's valour and success he treats him as an inferior, and is quite firm, though both Goneril and Regan bring forward their authority against him.

Question 5.

Compare and contrast the religious beliefs or superstitions of the principal characters in the play.

Answer

Although Shakespeare has laid his story in heathen times there is a definite lack of uniformity in the degree of faith the various characters show in the gods; ranging from the fervour of a strict religious nature in Edgar to scepticism in Edmund. *Edmund*, thrown into the world, sees nothing to believe in but Nature and the invention of his own brain —

"Thou, Nature, art my goddess; to thy law
    My services are bound."

And he despises those who believe in any supernatural power.

"This is the excellent foppery of the world, that when we are sick in fortune... we make guilty of our disasters the sun, the moon, and the stars: as if we were villains by necessity: fools by heavenly compulsion... and all that we are evil in, by a divine thrusting on."

In his last moments he expresses a belief in "fortune", as a power which over-rules man's fate, exclaiming as he lies wounded to death by Edgar —

"The wheel is come full circle; I am here."

Edgar stands out in contrast to his brother as the most religious person in the drama. In his reasoning on his own undeserved troubles and his attitude towards suffering in others, there is a tone of religious resignation and sympathy, and he is quick to credit the so-called chances of life to the powers above us. Thus he says to Gloucester, who supposes himself to have fallen from a precipice —

"Think that the clearest gods, who make them honours
    Of men's impossibilities, have preserved thee."

And thus he points out the justice of the gods in punishing Gloucester by the hand of Edmund —

"The gods are just, and of our pleasant vices
    Make instruments to plague us."

Goneril never mentions the gods; she is not actively sceptical like Edmund, but utterly irreligious. Her father's curses, which make *Regan* tremble and exclaim —

"O, the blest gods! So will you wish on me
    When the rash fit is on,"

108

in no way move her. In the same way, when the news reaches her that speedy vengeance has overtaken Cornwall, and when Albany says —

> "This shows you are above
> You justicers, that these our nether crimes
> So speedily can venge,"

Goneril just turns the matter over in her mind to examine how it will serve or hinder her own designs. *Regan*, more timid than her sister, brings to mind the words of St. James II, 19, "The devils also believe and tremble."

Cordelia believes in the gods as a matter of course, and the outcome of her belief is her beautiful character. She does not, like Edgar, talk religion; but, as Kent says, she thinks justly, and in all her words and actions shows a firm devotion to goodness. In the scene of her father's restoration after sleep, the scene in which we see her deeply moved, she asks the doctor to do all in his power to restore the king, and to his art she adds her prayer —

> "O you kind gods,
> Cure this great breach in his abused nature!
> The untuned and jarring senses, O, wind up
> Of this child-changed father."

Gloucester is religious, but he is also very superstitious. He credits Edgar's supposed villainy, the king's unnatural treatment of Cordelia, and Kent's banishment to

> "These late eclipses in the sun and moon."

Edmund, while he despises them, plays upon these feelings (Act I, Sc. 2), but *Edgar* makes use of them to help show his father how the gods have preserved him from destruction (Act IV, Sc. 6). Nearly his last words express his patient resignation to the will of the gods —

> "You ever gentle gods, take my breath from me;
> Let not my worser spirit tempt me again
> To die before you please."

Albany believes in the gods, as shown by his words quoted above; he seems to fear them as the avengers of evil. In the dark soul of *Cornwall* we can distinguish no spark of light, shed by either religious or superstitious belief.

The *Servants* in Gloucester's castle may be taken to represent the religious belief of the people generally, and in this connection their words, after witnessing the cruelty of Cornwall and Regan, are important: —
Second Servant —

> "I'll never care what wickedness I do,
> If this man come to good."

Third Servant —

"If she live long
And in the end meet the old course of death,
Women will all turn monsters."

Kent is more than tolerant towards the beliefs of others; to the king, swearing his determination by Apollo, he answers —

"Now, by Apollo, king,
Thou swear'st thy gods in vain,"

and in bidding farewell to all the Court, he blesses Cordelia with the words —

"The gods to their dear shelter take thee, maid."

Still Kent does not seem to feel with certainty that this world is over-ruled by the beneficent power of the gods. At one time (in the stocks in Gloucester's courtyard) we hear him appealing to *Fortune* as a power which guides the course of the world —

"Fortune, good night: smile once more; turn thy wheel."

At another time, when confronted by the difficulty of trying to reunite the three sisters, he says —

"It is the stars,
The stars above us govern our conditions."

But these questions do not really seem much to concern him; fidelity and loyalty are his religion.

Lear himself is always firm in his faith that the world is governed by the gods, and in justice; he calls on the gods to confirm his oaths —

"By Jupiter
This shall not be revoked."

He calls down curses from the gods on Goneril —

"Hear, nature, hear; dear goddess, hear!
Suspend thy purpose."

He does not question the will of the gods in letting him suffer from his daughters' unkindness, but prays —

"If it be you that stirs these daughters' hearts
Against their father, fool me not so much
To bear it tamely; touch me with noble anger."

Again, in the storm, sure of the justice of the gods, he prays them to —

"Find out their enemies now,"

and separates himself from evil doers, as having no cause to fear the wrath of the gods —

110

"I am a man,
More sinn'd against than sinning."

In one of his last speeches he declares his faith in the gods as the rewarders of goodness, saying to Cordelia, as they are being led to prison —

"Upon such sacrifices, my Cordelia,
  The gods themselves throw incense."

It seems worthwhile briefly to point out that, if on reading the tragedy of *King Lear* we are forced to ask, What power then rules the world? Good? Evil? or Chance? we may remember that Lear, the man whose sufferings were so heart-rendering that we can hardly bear to read of them, never had any doubt.

Question 6.

Discuss the Fool in *King Lear*.

Answer

Professor Bradley writes: "The Fool is one of Shakespeare's triumphs in *King Lear*. Imagine the tragedy without him, and you hardly know it. To remove him would spoil its harmony, as the harmony of a picture would be spoiled if one of the colours were extracted. One can almost imagine that Shakespeare, going home from an evening at the 'Mermaid', where he had listened to Jonson fulminating against fools in general, and perhaps criticising the Clown in *Twelfth Night* in particular, had said to himself: 'Come, my friends, I will show you once for all that the mischief is in you, and not in the fool or the audience. I will have a fool in the most tragic of my tragedies. He shall not play a little part. He shall keep from first to last the company in which you most object to see him, the company of a king. Instead of amusing the king's idle hours, he shall stand by him in the very tempest and whirlwind of passion. Before I have done you shall confess, between laughter and tears, that he is of the very essence of life, that you have known him all your days though you never recognized him till now, and that you would as soon go without Hamlet as miss him'."

The Fool has been called a sort of *outer conscience* to Lear, who awakens in his master a consciousness of his folly, and who, when Lear is fully convinced of this and of his unkindness towards Cordelia, drops out of the play, his work being accomplished. There may be some touch of truth in this idea; but surely there is none in the belief that his continual reminders to the king in joke, rhyme, or proverb are intended for a consistent course of torment; the king's evident tender affection for the Fool refutes such an idea. No, the Fool seems, like others who held such parts in kings' and great men's courts, to be a person (a youth, I think) of imperfect or abnormal brain power, and of a fragile bodily development, a creature who "pines away" when his young mistress is banished, and who is cowed and silent in the presence of Goneril and Regan. The first time we see him, when the result of the division of the kingdom and of Cordelia's banishment is beginning to be felt, we find his mind is possessed — to the exclusion of all else — by this one idea, and the folly of the king in bringing things to such a pass. At every available opportunity he thrusts in a reminder, untill we feel that he really has a share in goading his master to madness. But it is so natural for a person in his state to harp on one idea, and moreover the very purpose of his job is to turn everything to jest. This is what makes it so affecting to see him in the storm scenes making a tremendous effort to stop this carrying on and to comfort the king; and to hear him, when once he lapses into a rhyme on the old theme, follow it up quickly by the ridiculous picture of a pretty woman making faces in her glass. It is equally affecting, too, to see him when Lear has become mad, and is going to take off his clothes. Kent is shocked and does nothing, but the Fool goes up to his master with the words, "Prithee, nuncle, be contented; 't is a naughty night to swim in". In the farmhouse scene he gives us proof of his power of seeing what is hidden from others, in his being the only one who recognizes Edgar in his madman's rages; meaning Gloucester, he says, "He's a mad yeoman that sees his son a gentleman before him". After this scene we do not see the Fool again; and it is only natural to conclude that the exposure to the cold and wet on that awful night, together with the mental effort of sustaining a consistent course of action in comforting the king, was too much for his delicate frame; and his own words capping the mad Lear's "We'll go to supper i' the morning", (Fool) "And I'll go to bed at noon", sound like a prophecy of his own death.

There is one noticeable matter in Shakespeare's treatment of Lear's Fool, namely, that twice he prepares us for a gentle and loving reception of him just before he appears. The first occasion is that of his first appearance (in Act I), when in answer to the king's inquiry as to where he is, a knight replies, "Since my young lady's going into France, sir, the fool hath much pined away".

This at once brings us into sympathy with him as the only person in Goneril's palace who seems to mourn the loss of Cordelia. And the same feeling is experienced in Act III, when we hear that Lear is out in the storm "Contending with the fretful elements", and in reply to Kent's question, "Who is with him?" comes the answer —

"None but the fool; who labours to outjest
His heart-struck injuries."

Question 7.

What letters are received in the course of the action of the play? By whom were they sent? How do they help or explain the action of the play?

Answer

(a) The false letter which Edmund shows (as he pretends unwillingly) to Gloucester brings about Edgar's banishment, influences the subplot of the play throughout, and prepares the way for Edgar's championship of justice in both plots.

(b) The letter sent by Goneril to Regan, about the same time as the king sent one to her, effectively hardened Regan's heart, and rendered their father's appeal useless.

(c) We see Kent reading a letter from Cordelia, while he is in the stocks. This letter acts as dramatic relief, and as "comfortable beams" lighting up the darkness which seems to be closing around the king and those who remain faithful to him.

(d) Gloucester receives a letter, of which we do not know the writer. It contains information concerning the state of affairs in Britain, and perhaps news of the French invasion. It helps advance the catastrophe in the subplot, when through Edmund's treachery Cornwall is informed of it, and punishes Gloucester for this and the further *treason* of helping the king by plucking out his eyes.

It is this letter which is afterwards (Act III, Sc. 6) sent by Cornwall to Albany.

(e) Kent sent a letter by the gentleman to Cordelia, informing her of the king's miseries. It is important because of the account the gentleman gives of Cordelia's reception of it. In this way Shakespeare is given an opportunity to show us more of Cordelia's character.

(f) The letter sent to Edmund from Goneril by the hands of Oswald brought about the destruction of her evil plot, and provides the means by which Edgar is able to avenge his brother's treachery.

Question 8.

Give instances, quoting where you can, to show how Lear's mind is occupied with the thoughts of his daughters' ingratitude.

Answer

It is clear that the thought of Goneril's ingratitude is the cause of the outburst of passion which drives Lear from her home to Regan's. Twice in this scene he exclaims against filial ingratitude —

"Ingratitude, thou marble-hearted fiend,
  More hideous when thou show'st thee in a child,
  Than the sea-monster!"
"How sharper than a serpent's tooth it is
  To have a thankless child!"

In the following scene, where the king is setting out for Regan's palace, the same thought seems urging him on, and he bursts out with such words as —

"So kind a father"
. . . .
"To take 't again by perforce! Monster ingratitude!"

When he sees Regan he tells her of Goneril's treatment of him.

"She hath tied

Sharp-tooth'd unkindness, like a vulture, here.
All the stored vengeance of heaven fall
On her ingrateful top!"

He tells Regan, too, that she knows better the "dues of gratitude".

"Thy half of the kingdom hast thou not forgot,
Wherein I thee endow'd."

When the two daughters combine to deprive him of his train, he reminds them, "I gave you all".

We next see Lear in the storm, and there, as his mind is rapidly giving way, he dwells almost continuously on the ingratitude of his daughters. He forgives the elements for the misery they cause him, because, he says —

"I never gave you kingdom, call'd you daughters.
You owe me no subscription."

When Kent begs him to enter the hovel for shelter, he says it is better for him to be out in the raging storm, for there he does not feel so strongly the storm within his breast, and the cause of this inward storm again bursts from him —

"Filial ingratitude!
Is it not as this mouth should tear this hand
For lifting food to 't"

and,

"O, Regan, Goneril!
Your old kind father, whose frank heart gave all."

But the strongest and strangest proof of how this idea possesses the king is that, when he sees Edgar in his madman's rags, he at once thinks that he too has unfilial daughters who have brought him to this pass.

"Hast thou given all to thy two daughters?"

he asks him, and then —

"What, have his daughters brought him to this pass?
Could'st thou save nothing? Did'st thou give them all?"

and when Kent says "He has no daughters", Lear replies —

"Death, traitor! Nothing could have subdued nature to such a
lowness, but his unkind daughters."

In the scene in the farmhouse, where the king is raving mad, he thinks that he is trying his daughters for their ingratitude. He calls on those present to dissect Regan, and asks, "Is there any cause in nature, that makes these hard hearts?"

And at the end of the play when Lear is recovering from his madness with Cordelia's help, he recalls the cause of his problems and says, "Your sisters have, as I do remember, done me wrong."

Question 9.

Shakespeare frequently reveals a character to us in his or her first words. Show that this is done in the case of Cordelia.

Answer

The first words of Cordelia, which, since they are spoken to herself are more convincing, reveal an important trait in her character, that of deeply restrained feeling. After Goneril's extravagant declaration of love to their father Cordelia says aside. "What shall Cordelia do? Love and be silent," And we know what followed. When her turn came to "heave her heart into her mouth" she could say nothing. If we are ever inclined to think that it was "pride which she calls plainness" which prevented her from speaking her love true, we have only to turn to the scene in Act IV, where the king awakes from his long sleep and slowly regains consciousness. Then Cordelia wanted with all her being to restore her father by her love, but when he first wakes she asks the doctor to speak to him! And when she speaks herself she is able to say little, and her words sound forced. She longed to be received back as his daughter, but to her father's question, "I think this lady to be my child, Cordelia," she can only repeat, "And so I am; I am." And when he says he knows she has cause to hate him, she repeats again, "No cause, no cause".

Her restrained feeling is shown in other respects than in her affections. Note the restraint she shows when bidding farewell to her sisters; for although she knows them for what they are, and clearly (with wash'd eyes) sees their faults, she restrains her feelings of contempt. This is shown, too, when she speaks of her sisters in the last scene as "These sisters and these daughters". Again, when Cordelia hears particulars of her father's sufferings and her sisters' inhumanity, she restrains her feelings, not only of love and pity, but of horror. "She was queen over her passion," and "patience and sorrow strove, who could express her goodliest".

Question 10.

What is meant by dramatic background? How does the storm in Act III heighten the effect of the moral crisis and Lear's mental breakdown?

Answer

The term dramatic background means everything that we understand by the term surroundings; it includes scenery, atmosphere, and local colour.

The terrific tempest described in Act III — the most severe Kent had known for many years (note: "since I was man") — had considerable effect on the progress of Lear's mental breakdown, which, beginning with the heartless cruelty of his two daughters and the callousness of Cornwall, reached its climax with the appearance of the supposed Bedlamite. The picture of the old king "contending with the fretful elements" is one which fills us with feelings of pity and awe. We find him calling upon the winds to blow the earth into the sea, or to raise the curled waters to submerge the earth; upon the rain to flood the land until it cover the church steeples; upon the lightning to singe his white head; upon the thunder to shake the world to pieces "that things might change or cease". According to his varying moods he tries to out-scorn the wind and rain: calls on the gods to find out their enemies: appeals for pity —

"Here I stand your slave,
A poor, infirm, weak, and despised old man.
. . . .
I am a man
More sinn'd against than sinning:"

thinks of revenge,

"But I will punish home,
No; I will weep no more:"

declares that he will be the pattern of all patience; that the tempest in his mind is more terrible than that raging in the outside world; and through it all, the thought of those monsters of ingratitude is ever present in his mind mingling with or over-mastering his bodily misery —

"Nor rain, wind, thunder, fire, are my daughters."
"Filial ingratitude."
"In such a night as this! O Regan, Goneril!
Your old kind father whose frank heart gave all."

Etc., etc.

The storm also accents, and, to some extent, causes the alterations in Lear's manner of regarding his fellow man. "Sweet are the uses of adversity", how it all helps to bring about the moral regeneration. His fool seems to him now an object of pity. "How dost, my boy, art cold?" and he seeks the hovel far more to relieve the suffering of the fool than for his own sake; and just before his mind finally gives way he talks about the miseries of the wretched in what he calls his prayer before sleep.

Bibliography

Burckhardt, Sigurd. "The Quality of Nothing." *Shakespearean Meanings*, pp. 237-59. Princeton: Princeton University Press, 1968. A brilliant essay on the mediate vs. the immediate in the characters, experiences, and presentation of Lear and Gloucester.

Chambers, R.W. *King Lear*. Glasgow: Jackson, Son & Company, 1940. A reading of the play stressing the victory of love and refuting more pessimistic critics by pointing out that Shakespeare has mitigated the final horror of the many versions of the *Lear* story in which Cordelia commits suicide.

Clemen, Wolfgang H. *The Development of Shakespeare's Imagery*, pp. 133-53. Cambridge: Harvard University Press, 1951. An examination of the dramatic function of imagery in *Lear*, as well as the implications of particular image patterns.

Colie, Rosalie L. *Paradoxia Epidemica: The Renaissance Tradition of Paradox*, pp. 261-81. Princeton: Princeton University Press, 1966. Emphasizes the fusion and interplay of traditional paradoxes in *Lear*, as well as their nontraditional effect of drawing "the beholder into the experience of contradiction."

Colie, Rosalie L. and F.T. Flahiff, eds. *Some Facets of "King Lear": Essays in Prismatic Criticism*. Toronto: University of Toronto Press, 1974. An excellent collection of essays from diverse points of view.

Coursen, Herbert R., Jr. *Christian Ritual and the World of Shakespeare's Tragedies*, pp. 237-313. Lewisburg: Bucknell University Press, 1976. An extensive discussion of Christian analogues and echoes in *Lear*. Coursen argues that the hints of Christian redemption serve only to underscore the bleakness of the end.

Doran, Madeleine. "Command, Questions, and Assertion in *King Lear*." *In Shakespeare's Art*, edited by Milton Crane, pp. 53-78. Chicago: University of Chicago Press, 1973. Discusses the significance of these three syntactical forms in creating the world of the play; particularly interesting in noting the relative absence of the conditional except in the speech of the fool, who tries to teach Lear about the world of contingency.

Empson, William. "Fool in *Lear*." *The Structure of Complex Words*, pp. 125-57. London: Chatto & Windus, 1951. A quirky and suggestive essay on folly emphasizing its dark side: Lear as clown and imbecile, and the heavens as fools who make fools of man.

Everett, Barbara. "The New *King Lear*." *Critical Quarterly*, 2 (1960), 325-39. An analysis of the genesis and consequences of criticism stressing the "reconciliation" at the end of *Lear*; she argues for a view of the play dependent on a tragic valuation of life and its losses.

117

Frost, William. "Shakespeare's Rituals and the Opening Scene of *King Lear.*" *Hudson Review*, 10 (1957-58), 577-85. An influential discussion of ritualistic elements in Act I, Scene 1 and the effect of the breakdown of ritual throughout the play.

Granville-Barker, Harley. *Prefaces to Shakespeare*, I, 261-334. Princeton: Princeton University Press, 1946. A thorough refutation of the Lamb-Bradley notion that *Lear* is better suited to the study than the stage; Granville-Barker demonstrates that structure, style, and character work toward specifically dramatic ends.

Heilman, Robert Bechtold. *This Great Stage: Image and Structure in "King Lear."* Seattle: University of Washington Press, 1963. Originally published in 1948, this is the classic study of patterns of image and theme in the play. Heilman traces patterns associated with sight, clothing, nature, justice, values, madness, reason, and the gods. The emphasis is on the redemptive paradoxes of the play.

Holland, Norman N. *Psychoanalysis and Shakespeare.* New York: McGraw-Hill, 1966. A guide to a variety of psychoanalytic interpretations of Shakespeare. Holland's own interpretation of *Lear* emphasizes the importance of masochistic strategies as attempts to buy love by a form of prepayment in suffering.

Kernan, Alvin B. "Formalism and Realism in Elizabethan Drama: the Miracles in *King Lear.*" *Renaissance Drama*, 9 (1966), 59-66. A discussion of Shakespeare's exploitation of the tension between formalism and realism, particularly in Gloucester's mock suicide; Kernan sees this scene as Edgar's morality play in which the "miracles" are partly true but partly undercut by the theatrical absurdity.

Kott, Jan. "King Lear or Endgame." *Shakespeare Our Contemporary,* pp. 87-124. Garden City: Doubleday & Company, Inc., 1964. Despite its exaggerations and omissions, this essay is sometimes suggestive about the affinities of *Lear* with mime and theater of the absurd. It is moreover significant in having helped to shape the conception behind one of the greatest and most controversial stage productions of the twentieth century, the Peter Brook *King Lear.* (For an illuminating discussion of the successes and failures of this production and the interpretation behind it, see V.A. Kolve, "The modernity of *Lear*," *in Pacific Coast Studies in Shakespeare*, edited by Waldo F. McNeir and Thelma N. Greenfield, pp. 173-89. Eugene: University of Oregon Books, 1966).

Maxwell, J.C. "The Technique of Invocation in *King Lear.*" *Modern Language Review*, 45 (1950), 142-47. One of the earliest essays to trace the ways in which each character's "religion" reflects his own nature, as well as the progress of Lear and Gloucester toward Christian attitudes.

Stockholder, Katherine. "The Multiple Genres of *King Lear:* Breaking the Archetypes." *Bucknell Review*, 16 (1968), 40-63. A study of the tensions produced by the elements of fairy tale, farce, and satiric comedy that combine with tragedy in *Lear*.